"The journey out of and b   n
complex and challenging. W   a
meaningful roadmap for that very journey. While deeply grounded in recent
evidence and her own research, readers of this book will find compassionate
and practical guidance for moving forward with their lives after an abusive
relationship. This book is recommended for those working to end a violent
relationship, those who are recently coming out of a violent relationship, and
for those who love someone struggling with a violent relationship, whether
you are parent, sibling, new partner, or friend."

—**Rebecca J. Macy**, Ph.D., MSW, L. Richardson Preyer
Distinguished Chair for Strengthening Families,
Associate Dean for Research and Faculty Development,
Editor-in-Chief *Journal of Family Violence*

"*Triumph Over Abuse: Healing, Recovery, and Purpose after an Abusive Relationship*
by Dr. Christine Murray is a thorough, comprehensive and practical guide
for victims and survivors of intimate partner violence. Dr. Murray crafted
this book in such a way that the experience of reading it feels very much like
talking with an old friend who has 'been there' and knows how to guide a
victim/survivor through the thought process and behavioral choices aimed
at reclaiming their life after the end of an abusive relationship. In addition to
her own voice, Dr. Murray represents the voices of countless other victims
and survivors who have shared their experiences and insights in the research
she has done on strategies used to heal from the wounds of intimate partner
violence. In addition to survivors, this book should be read by every person
who works with victims and survivors because it places the helper in the
shoes of the victim/survivor and provides the means for respectful, trauma
informed thinking and communication. At every step, Dr. Murray describes
the issue at hand, discusses options and affirms the reader's right to decide for
themselves how, when and whether to proceed. This is a wonderful resource
and I will use it in my own work with intimate partner violence survivors."

—**L. Kevin Hamberger**, Ph.D., Professor of Family and
Community Medicine, Medical College of Wisconsin

Triumph Over Abuse

In this book Christine Murray carefully weaves her personal experiences as a survivor with her professional expertise as a counselor, community advocate, and researcher into a comprehensive guidebook for survivors of abuse.

Moving forward after suffering abuse at the hands of someone who is supposed to love and care for you is no easy feat. And yet, healing and recovering from past abuse is possible, and the journey to get there can be an empowering opportunity for growth. *Triumph Over Abuse* provides a road map for doing more than simply moving on from the past. Filled with accessible case studies and exercises, the book offers extensive practical guidance on a range of topics, such as building coping skills, surrounding yourself with the right kinds of support, working through traumatic memories, and channeling your experience into helping others and making a difference in the world.

The book will inspire and equip survivors of abuse to build full, meaningful lives despite the trauma they have faced, as well as being a tool for clinicians to use to support clients.

Christine E. Murray, Ph.D., LCHMC, LMFT, is the Director of the UNC Greensboro Center for Youth, Family, and Community Partnerships. She is a co-founder of the See the Triumph campaign.

Triumph Over Abuse

Healing, Recovery, and Purpose after an Abusive Relationship

CHRISTINE E. MURRAY

12/31/2020

Dear Rebecca,
Thank you so much
for your support of this
book and for all you
do to support survivors!
Christine

Routledge
Taylor & Francis Group

NEW YORK AND LONDON

First published 2021
by Routledge
52 Vanderbilt Avenue, New York, NY 10017

and by Routledge
2 Park Square, Milton Park, Abingdon, Oxon, OX14 4RN

Routledge is an imprint of the Taylor & Francis Group, an informa business

Library of Congress Cataloging-in-Publication Data
Names: Murray, Christine E., author.
Title: Triumph over abuse: healing, recovery, and purpose after an
abusive relationship/Christine E. Murray, Ph.D., LCMH, LMFT.
Description: New York, NY: Routledge, 2021. | Includes bibliographical
references and index.
Identifiers: LCCN 2020035504 (print) | LCCN 2020035505 (ebook) |
ISBN 9780367635534 (hardback) | ISBN 9780367646455 (paperback) |
ISBN 9781003125624 (ebook)
Subjects: LCSH: Victims of family violence. | Family violence. | Intimate
partner violence.
Classification: LCC HV6626 .M873 2021 (print) | LCC HV6626 (ebook) |
DDC 616.85/82203–dc23
LC record available at https://lccn.loc.gov/2020035504
LC ebook record available at https://lccn.loc.gov/2020035505

ISBN: 978-0-367-63553-4 (hbk)
ISBN: 978-0-367-64645-5 (pbk)
ISBN: 978-1-003-12562-4 (ebk)

Typeset in Dante MT Std
by KnowledgeWorks Global Ltd.

This book is dedicated to my sons, Evan and Bryce.
I am thankful for your love, support, and laughs.

Contents

Acknowledgements

This book was on my heart to write for many years before I finally found the courage and motivation to write it. In fact, it went from my heart onto the page as an outline about a year before I even started the actual writing. Finding the right timing to write this book was a challenge on many levels, and it wasn't just a scheduling issue. I knew I wanted to share parts of my own story as part of this book, and I needed to figure out the right time and way to do that before I could really start writing the book.

With that in mind, I owe all thanks for this book to the many people who've supported me both professionally in my work related to abuse recovery, as well as personally in my own journey as a survivor of abuse myself.

Throughout my career, I've learned so much from many professionals who are on the frontlines of responding to violence and abuse in the community. I'm especially grateful to the staff and partners of the Guilford County Family Justice Center, and I commit to donate a portion of all proceeds from this book to support their good work.

I also gratefully acknowledge all who are currently or formerly part of the See the Triumph campaign community, especially my co-founder, Dr. Allison Crowe. Without the research and outreach done related to the See the Triumph campaign, this book would not have been possible.

I am also very thankful to colleagues at the University of North Carolina who've supported and encouraged my passion for bridging research and practice to support people whose lives have been impacted by unsafe, abusive relationships. Thanks especially to Dr. Terri Shelton for being so supportive of my desire to bring my own experiences and story into my work so soon after starting my new job under her supervision.

On a personal level, I am grateful to all my friends and family members who have helped me along the way of my own journey toward triumphing over abuse, as well as for your ongoing, unwavering support of my career and my family. Your encouragement has meant more than you could ever know. I also want to thank my sons, Evan and Bryce, for all the ways you inspire me and keep me laughing.

Finally, above all else, this book is the result of the many insights about abuse and the recovery process I've learned from survivors, whether through research, other aspects of my work, or from friends or family who've shared their stories with me. I only hope this book does justice to honor the power of your stories and your strength.

1
INTRODUCTION
Triumphing Over Abuse

"Don't ever think you're a victim because you have the power to move from being abused to being a survivor ... a smarter, stronger and more beautifully resilient version of you than you ever imagined!"

~ Domestic Violence Survivor

"You are a victim until you decide to acknowledge that a victim is what you were and a survivor is what you want to be. There is a lot of work that survivors do to become healthy, functioning members of society and they are seldom, if ever, given the credit they deserve. We should be able to wear the badge of survivor with honor, it should not be something we feel carries a stigma."

~ Domestic Violence Survivor

Going through an abusive relationship changes you. While you're in an abusive relationship, the changes you see in yourself can feel completely negative—you may feel weak, lose your self-esteem, feel at fault for the abuse, feel alone, or feel less than other people. Often, this is what society says about people in abusive relationships—that there must be "something wrong with them" to end up in that situation. In this book, my goal is to help flip that script for people who've experienced abuse and help them reclaim their right to healthy, fulfilling lives and relationships.

What if, instead of viewing people who've been abused as weak, we began to celebrate the strength it takes to persevere while overcoming the harm that was placed on them by someone who was supposed to love and care for them? What if, instead of accepting the myth that there's something wrong with people who were abused, we place full responsibility and accountability for the abuse on the people who perpetrate it? If you've been in an abusive relationship, my goals in this book are to help you release shame, see the full magnitude of your strength, and understand your abuser's responsibility for the hurt they created in your life—even if they won't acknowledge any of it.

Freedom and hope are possible in the aftermath of abuse, although the recovery journey can be a long and difficult one. There can be lingering consequences from abuse that may affect you for years to come, such as physical pain, mental health symptoms, financial setbacks, and stress from ongoing abuse, especially if you share custody of children with your abuser. One or more of these lasting consequences of abuse can cause a lot of challenges, and this book offers practical suggestions for working through these challenges on the path to recovery.

Even in the face of ongoing challenges, survivors can embrace positive opportunities, personal strengths, and a renewed sense of purpose in life. The changes that can come from going through abuse can include positive ones—including the chance to reclaim a brighter future for yourself, as well as others in your life, including children, friends, family, and your community. Abuse is about power and control, and when you were being abused, there was a lot about your life that was out of your control. The aftermath of the abuse is your opportunity to regain control of your own life and figure out how you can use that self-determination to make a powerful difference in the world around you. You can not only be a *survivor* of past abuse, but you also can *triumph* over abuse and build a beautiful future.

What Does It Mean to Triumph over Abuse?

Generally speaking, I use the term *victim* to refer to someone who is currently involved in an abusive relationship, and I use the term *survivor* to refer to someone who has faced abuse in the past but is no longer currently at-risk for abuse. However, these terms are tricky for a number of reasons. Some people don't like the term *victim* because it implies weakness, although others prefer the term because it acknowledges the harm being done by another person. The term *victim* also reflects that many forms of abuse are illegal, criminal behavior. The term *survivor* also certainly could be applied to people who are surviving current abuse, and in reality, for many survivors, just because an abusive relationship has ended does not mean that the abuse itself stops. Many survivors face ongoing abuse for many years following the official end of an abusive relationship, as we'll discuss in detail in Chapter 8.

Although I like the term *survivor* and even embrace this term personally (as I'll share more with you later in this chapter), I've always found the term to be somewhat limiting. It's a strong word that implies that you've overcome challenges, but merely surviving something also could just mean you've simply gotten through it. If someone is a victim when they're being abused, then a survivor after they've gotten through it, what comes next?

There are many possible ways to describe life post-abuse. One of the beautiful things about the empowerment approach that underlies most services for people who've faced abuse is that each person should be empowered to make choices about their own lives. This is my first practical tip for you: take time to consider what identity in terms of victim, survivor, or something else fits most for you. Ultimately, we're all unique, whole people whose lives are impacted by the sum of our experiences. It's okay to not embrace the term *survivor,* and to say, "I'm me!"

I'll use the term survivor throughout this book, however, and I think it's useful language that we can use to refer to a shared experience of being someone who has faced past abuse. If you're currently involved in an abusive relationship, I hope this book will be of use to you as you think forward to your future life, although the main audience this book is written for is those on the journey of recovering from past abuse.

The word *triumph* is one of the best I've heard to describe the process of fully overcoming past abuse. This word has special meaning to me, as it's included in the name of the research-based social media campaign I co-founded with my colleague, Dr. Allison Crowe. We launched See the Triumph (www.seethetriumph.org) on January 1, 2013, with the mission of ending the stigma surrounding intimate partner violence and creating supportive resources for survivors. The campaign grew out of our research to understand the stigma surrounding intimate partner violence. We've done a series of research studies related to See the Triumph for nearly 10 years. To date, we've been grateful to over 1,250 survivors of past abuse who've shared their stories with us. You'll learn more about this research throughout this book, and the participants in this research are the ones who shared the quotes that you'll find at the start of each chapter.

We named the campaign "See the Triumph" because the phrase was shared by one of the earliest participants in our research. She experienced horrific physical and verbal abuse at the hands of her former boyfriend. When I interviewed her, she told us that people had asked her if she was embarrassed about the abuse she experienced. Her response was so powerful:

> The only thing that bothers me about it is that other people can't see the triumph in it. Because to me this is a treasure to be at this point in my life, in this stage, and it be beginning. Some people don't even start to realize that they have the issues or start dealing with them until they get to this point.

As this quote illustrates, people often overlook the triumphs involved in overcoming past abuse. But every triumph—big and small—carries a victory over some element of the negativity of abuse. Triumphing over abuse means a process of claiming victories over the abuse and overcoming to a point that the abuse no longer is the dominating force in your life. Triumphing over abuse doesn't require complete and perfect healing—nor does it require any one specific formula for the healing journey. It allows survivors to claim their own personal victories and determine the path their lives will take for themselves. I want you to keep this point in mind as you read through the rest of this book—any and all suggestions I offer are merely options to consider whether they would be helpful and applicable to you. Every person's path is unique, and I encourage you to consider these suggestions and apply those that make sense to you, but also disregard those that don't seem like a good fit for your life and your unique circumstances.

For people who experienced being controlled by an abuser, having freedom to self-determine your own life can be difficult at first. I've spoken with survivors who were overwhelmed by the process of learning about themselves—they didn't even know things like what kind of food they like, what they like to do for fun, and how they want to spend their time. If you've been controlled by another person for a long time, it's natural to feel overwhelmed by your new-found freedom. Keep in mind that there's no set timeline for healing and triumphing over abuse. Move at your own pace, and take one step at a time.

Over time, the earliest steps toward recovering from past abuse often become giant strides, and each person's path is unique. From the beginning, I want to emphasize that there's not one prescription for what the end goal of that journey will be that fits all people. For some people, the journey evolves into becoming a professional advocate who works daily to help others affected by abuse. Others prefer to distance themselves from the issue and don't get involved in abuse-related causes in any way. Both of these paths—and anything in between—can be healthy, so long as it's the path you choose for yourself and it's one that feels healthy, safe, and meaningful to you.

A Little Bit About Me

We're about to embark on a journey together throughout this book, so I want to share a bit about me so you'll understand the background for the ideas contained in the book. Professionally, my passion for almost two decades now has been work related to intimate partner violence and other forms of interpersonal violence and abuse. My background is in the counseling field, and some of my earliest counseling experiences were working with people whose lives had been deeply impacted by abuse. I wasn't even working in a domestic violence agency, but I estimated at least 90 percent of the clients I served in an adult outpatient mental health treatment facility had experienced current or past abuse. In client after client, I saw how their experiences with the trauma of abuse had a profound influence on their lives, and many of them hadn't received the proper support to help them effectively heal from the trauma they faced.

After working full-time as a counselor, I moved into the world of academia and became a professor for 14 years in a counseling department, where I taught about couple and family counseling—including teaching a graduate-level class on family violence for many years—and focused the majority of my research on anything and everything related to violence and abuse. In addition to the research related to the See the Triumph campaign that I described above, other topics I've studied include how people cope with current abuse, gaps between research and practice in the domestic violence service field, community-based intervention strategies, batterer intervention programs, traumatic brain injury among domestic violence victims and survivors, geographic and neighborhood influences on domestic violence, and dating violence among teenagers and college students. I truly have tried to look at this issue from every angle so I can understand as much as possible about how people are impacted by abuse and what can be done to best support victims and survivors. In addition to my research, I've also been deeply engaged in community-level efforts to raise awareness about violence and abuse, as well as support the establishment of new supportive resources in our community, especially through involvement with our local Family Justice Center.

Recently, I moved to a new role within my university, and I'm now the director of a research center that bridges research and practice to address pressing social issues impacting youth and families. My recent work also has shifted upstream to more of a focus on promoting healthy relationships, and since 2015, I've been working on a community-wide campaign to promote happy, healthy, safe relationships of all kinds. By promoting healthy relationships, we aim to prevent relationship distress and abuse. Through this work, I've seen that a lot of people simply don't have the tools needed to build healthy relationships and are therefore more vulnerable to being at risk for experiencing abuse.

Hopefully, you can see my passion for the work that I do, and I've been fortunate to have many great professional experiences that informed my views on the abuse recovery process. Even with all of these professional experiences, some of the most valuable learning experiences I've had on this topic have come through my own personal experiences with healing and recovering from a past abusive relationship in my own life.

Many years ago, I myself was involved in an abusive intimate relationship. My abuser was a man that I loved, trusted, and was committed to. I'm fortunate the relationship is now many years in the past, but I can personally attest to the lengthy, and often grueling, process of recovering from abuse. I'll weave some of my experiences throughout this book when it's helpful to illustrate some of my points, so you'll learn more as you read on, but please keep in mind as you read this book that I'm on this journey of the process of triumphing over abuse right along with you. There's power in knowing we're not alone on this journey, and that many others have shared similar experiences.

It would be almost impossible for me to separate out what I've learned through my professional experiences and through my own personal journey. For most of the topics we'll discuss, I could likely share examples of research, describe theories, and provide examples of stories from my own life and from the survivors who shared their stories in our See the Triumph research. What's most important to me, however, is boiling the information down in a way that offers you guidance and practical tools for your personal journey. I hope you'll gain insights and tips for taking the next steps in your own path toward triumphing over abuse.

Overview of the Book

I've organized the chapters in this book so that we start with general topics, and then move into more specific challenges that can arise along the journey of recovering from past abuse. We'll start in Chapter 2 with a focus on self-care, and I encourage you to start there by building a personal toolkit of coping resources. In Chapter 3, we'll move into discussing how to surround yourself with the right type of social support, which for some survivors also can mean removing yourself from toxic relationships that hinder your growth. Chapter 4 will cover the importance of educating yourself about abuse as part of the healing journey so that you can better understand your own experiences and will clear up some common misconceptions about abuse.

In Chapter 5, we'll shift our focus toward taking back control of your mind following abuse. The process of breaking free from an abuser's mental control can be challenging, but it's an important step in the recovery journey. From there, we'll shift to fostering positive mental and emotional health in Chapter 6, including tips for finding a professional counselor who can support you and who understands the dynamics of abuse and trauma.

We'll turn to parenting issues in Chapter 7. Even if you don't have children, you may find this chapter helps you understand some of the parenting-related experiences that other survivors face. Parenting in the context of an abusive relationship can be highly complex, and custody issues can present special challenges. Relatedly, Chapter 8 addresses how to deal with continued abuse, which can involve custody issues, but also other potential legal issues even when children aren't involved, as well as other abuse tactics, like smearing your reputation and stalking or harassment. In Chapter 9, we'll cover the topics of finances, careers, and education, both in terms of understanding the impacts of abuse, and also to encourage you to dream and set goals in these areas of life.

The final section of the book will move to considering how survivors might want to be involved in helping others impacted by abuse (Chapter 10) and sharing their stories—on their own terms (Chapter 11). The book concludes with some final thoughts on taking a long-range view of life beyond the experience of abuse.

Overall, my goal in this book is to inspire, support, and challenge you to think through who you want to become as you envision your future life and move along your journey of recovering from (and triumphing over) abuse. As you move forward along this journey, keep an open mind, and don't let yourself be limited by what you've been told about who you are by your abuser or anyone else. Be watchful for your own self-expectations and how they may limit what you think is possible for your life.

Now is the time for you to begin to dream again! It may be necessary to learn to manage some negative lasting consequences of the abuse you've experienced, but you can also work toward transforming even the lingering negative effects into something positive for your life and the world around you. Remember that your journey is your own, and everyone reading this book will have a unique "finish line" they're working toward with respect to healing from and overcoming abuse.

Know that you don't have to become a vocal speaker or victim advocate for your life and experiences to have meaning and make a difference in the world. Even seemingly smaller missions—such as being a good mom, being a good friend, or simply learning to take care of yourself in life—are important and make an impact on the world. As you move along your journey to recovering from past abuse, you'll likely find that you'll have many opportunities ahead to make a difference, help others, and fulfill your own dreams.

As this journey begins, know that it's natural for some difficult emotions to come up as we address the topics covered in this book. To help prepare for this and other challenges along the way, let's get started in the next chapters with setting yourself up to practice self-care and build the right kind of support.

2
PRACTICING SELF-CARE AND COPING

"The relationship began when I was 18 and he was 34. He made me believe he loved me. He had affairs with other women during the course of our marriage. I raised his children from his first marriage. I also took care of both of his parents in their final months and days of life. I spent a lot of time trying to do 'better' so he would love and care for me, only to realize no human could have done more or 'better' than I did. Now, I'm enjoying taking care of myself."

~ Domestic Violence Survivor

As a counselor, one of the most important core principles to follow when working with a client who experienced any form of trauma is to make sure they've built up their coping resources enough that they're in a good place to address the emotionally-intense work of talking about and working through traumatic memories. This book isn't a counseling experience, of course, but the same principle is useful to consider as we start our journey through this book. There will be more difficult topics to work through later in the book, especially related to specific experiences and consequences of abuse. So, before we move to those more difficult topics, let's start by making sure you're ready to move forward into the more emotionally-intense work in the abuse recovery process.

Being "ready" to address traumatic memories and experiences isn't easy to define, so I encourage you to take it slowly and carefully observe your reactions. It's okay to take a step back if things become too intense, and there also may be times when your progress moves more quickly than you would have anticipated. There's not a set time-line recovering from abuse, so go at your own pace and allow yourself to take all the time you need to work through each step. This is your journey, so decide what pace and process will work best for you.

Self-care has become a popular buzzword, and we all realize the importance of taking at least some time to practice self-care and prioritize our well-being. We can't all afford to take a week-long spa vacation, but we all can commit to at least taking simple steps to care for ourselves, even if some days it means simply taking one minute to breathe calmly and reflect on life. Self-care in the aftermath of abuse can be complicated. Sometimes, it's difficult for survivors to relax, as a relaxed state can trigger emotional memories of past abuse. Even the concept of prioritizing yourself can be difficult to embrace for survivors who've been told their needs don't matter. And, sometimes the crises involved in abuse can put people into survival mode, so the thought of adding "self-care" to their to-do list seems like an unattainable goal. To get started with planning for how you can practice self-care in the context of your experiences with abuse, I'll introduce two concepts: the Trauma Backpack and the Coping Toolbox.

The Trauma Backpack

I'm an avid runner and hiker, and I've always thought that there are many parallels between long-distance endurance sports and the abuse recovery process. Recovering from past abuse is a marathon, not a sprint. With sprinting, a runner goes all out for a short period of time, burning through their energy as fast as they can. But long-distance running requires a different strategy–preserving your strength and energy for the final miles. Whether you run a marathon quickly or slowly, you still get from the start to the finish line one step at a time.

When you're covering a lot of miles—whether literally or metaphorically in the journey of triumphing over abuse—it's wise to travel as light as possible. However, when people have gone through a traumatic experience like abuse, the effects of that trauma can weigh them down. Picture yourself running a marathon with a backpack on your back. You'd want the backpack to weigh as little as possible, right? If you had to choose between running with a 50-pound or a 5-pound backpack, I'm pretty sure you'd choose the 5-pound backpack. In races and in life, we all want to make even uncomfortable situations feel as comfortable as possible.

Carrying around the effects of traumatic experiences in life can feel like carrying around a heavy backpack that weighs you down. Because each person responds to and is impacted by trauma in unique ways, the contents of every person's "trauma backpack" will vary as well. Some things you may be carrying include post-traumatic stress disorder (PTSD), depression, self-doubt, difficult memories, unanswerable questions ("Why did they do that to me?"), loneliness, stress from co-parenting with an abuser, unmet expectations, disappointment, unforgiveness, the challenges of being a single parent, guilt, and/or anger). I encourage you to reflect on the following two questions:

1. Am I carrying around a Trauma Backpack?
2. If so, what am I carrying, and how much is it weighing me down?

Later in the book, we'll start unpacking the various items that survivors often carry around after abuse. For now, I invite you to consider ways that your experiences with abuse are impacting your life now, as this can impact your coping and self-care. Some people who've faced abuse are able to move on from that experience and not have too much of a lingering burden to carry from it. However, most people who've gone through abuse carry around some effects, although the amount of the burden varies from person to person. Many factors impact this, including the severity, frequency, and duration of the abuse, resilience factors, social support, prior traumatic experiences, and how much stigma and victim-blaming a person experienced. To help you begin to understand what you may be carrying as a result of your experiences of being abused, complete Exercise 1.

One important aspect of the Trauma Backpack is that the backpack is contained. You know it's there, but the contents can be kept in the pack until it's time to take them out to work through them. You may not yet feel like the contents of your Trauma Backpack are contained if they spill over into your life, but consider how this image of a backpack can help you feel more intentional about how you respond to those effects of abuse. It's important to understand what's in there, because the amount of un-addressed "stuff" in your backpack represents how much you're weighed down as you go about

Exercise 1: My Trauma Backpack

Instructions: If you feel like you're carrying a "Trauma Backpack" with you, use the exercise below as an opportunity to reflect on ways your experiences with abuse are impacting you today.

First, imagine what your Trauma Backpack looks like. Is it large or small? How many sections does it contain? If it would be helpful to you, draw a picture representing your Trauma Backpack on a separate sheet of paper.

Next, write short words or phrases below to represent as many of the lingering effects of the abuse you experienced that you carry with you today. Examples may include mental health symptoms, loneliness, self-blame, financial stress, and physical pain. However, your backpack's contents will be unique to you, so take time to think about what is most weighing you down as a result of the abuse.

Second, consider that a Trauma Backpack could weigh anywhere from 1 pound, representing very little impact of the past abuse, to 100 pounds, representing the highest amount of abuse-related burdens possible. In the space below, write how much *your* trauma backpack weighs between 1 to 100 pounds.

My Trauma Backpack feels like it weighs _____ pounds.

Finally, in the space below, write a few sentences about how it feels to be carrying around your Trauma Backpack in your day-to-day life.

your daily life, as well as while you strive to create a better future for yourself. Unpacking the backpack over time is important, but before you get there, it's important to build your coping resources so you'll have many tools at your disposal to work through some of the challenges that lie ahead. So, now that we've acknowledged the Trauma Backpack, let's imagine setting it to the side for the time being while we focus on building another container—but this one will be filled with healthy tools to help you cope.

The Coping Toolbox

Coping skills are some of the most important life skills anyone can develop—whether or not they have a history of trauma. Even in the best-case scenario, challenges are a part of life. Coping skills help people work through difficult experiences, emotions, and challenges. These skills benefit everyone, but they're especially useful for people who've experienced trauma. Because the recovery process often involves unpacking, examining, and working through various aspects of the abuse and its consequences, it can lead to difficult emotions and stress. Coping skills help ensure you'll have the resources needed to work through these emotions so you can effectively navigate through them.

Let's turn our focus to helping you build a personalized Coping Toolbox that will be filled with coping tools and skills that can help you navigate through difficult times. Just as each person's Trauma Backpack has unique contents, so too will each person's Coping Toolbox. The coping strategies that work for each person are different, so it's important to experiment and see what works for you. For example, some people love quiet meditation as a coping and stress reduction strategy, whereas others find it stress-inducing to try and quiet their minds. As long as a coping tool has healthy, positive effects for you, that's what matters. Also keep in mind that some coping strategies that didn't work for you in the past may be helpful now. So, even if you tried something before and didn't like it, consider giving it another try now or in the future.

Unlike a Trauma Backpack, which weighs you down, a Coping Toolbox has the opposite effect: more tools in the box actually help make your load lighter. Different types of challenges in life call for different types of coping strategies. Coping with an immediate stressful situation, such as facing your abuser during a custody exchange, requires one approach, but longer-term issues, such as working through traumatic memories, requires another. That's why the idea of a Coping Toolbox is so useful. If you're doing home repairs, you need different tools for different tasks. No matter how expensive a hammer may be, it won't help at all if the job requires a wrench. As we discuss the many different possible coping tools you could use below, consider which ones might be helpful for addressing different challenges you face, especially as you think back to the contents of your Trauma Backpack.

Caution Against Maladaptive Coping Strategies

Sometimes, people use strategies they think are helping them cope with a difficult situation—and in fact, those strategies might help them feel better in the moment. But, some attempts at coping lead to negative consequences in the long run. Some of these are more obvious—such as using drugs to numb emotional pain. Sometimes, the line is a bit blurrier. For example, some people may find that drinking a glass of wine or two with a good friend is a nice way to relax and unwind. However, turning to alcohol as a coping strategy can become unhealthy if it happens too much or too often. It's not just substances that can be problematic—some other ways that people try to cope but that can have negative consequences include overspending, risky sexual activities, spending time with people who are toxic, and overusing social media.

One useful question you can ask yourself to consider the health of coping strategies you're using is the following:

> Is this thing I'm doing helping me work through my problems, or am I using this as a distraction that keeps me from addressing my problems?

Taking breaks and having some level of distraction from problems can be a useful tool, especially if it helps you come back to the problem later with a clearer mind and more ready to work through the problem. However, some distractions are used to avoid addressing problems overall. It's useful to examine if something that you're doing in an effort to cope is creating secondary problems in your life. For example, some people enjoy shopping as a bit of "retail therapy" to help them cope. To some, this could provide a way to temporarily take their mind off of their problems, and taking time to relax is beneficial. However, there's a big difference between purchasing an item that's in your budget and overspending to a point that puts you into debt and leads to financial stress.

If you're concerned that a particular strategy you're using might be turning into an unhelpful coping tool or creating secondary problems in your life, consider setting limits to help you stay on the healthy side of coping. Examples of limits might be sticking to no more than two glasses of wine, only shopping when you can afford to spend a certain amount within your budget, and limiting the amount of time you spend on social media. It also can be helpful to find an accountability partner in a trusted friend or family member to be honest with you to help you examine potentially concerning coping strategies you're using. Professional support also can be helpful, especially if you're noticing secondary problems arising from your attempts to cope through risky or unhealthy activities.

Building Your Coping Toolbox

I'm not the handiest person, so I don't have a lot of tools in my home. I have a small, pink toolbox with just the essentials, such as a hammer, screwdriver, pliers, and measuring tape. Even with such a small toolbox, it's hard to shut it when my tools are disorganized. Have you ever seen someone who has a lot of tools but keeps them disorganized, whether in a box, shed, or workbench? Usually, they can never find the tool they need, and it leads to a lot more frustration when trying to finish a job that requires a certain tool.

The Coping Window

Whether we're talking about tools like hammers and wrenches or tools for coping, it's useful to have a framework for organizing your toolbox so it'll be easier to find the right tool when you need it. That's why, several years ago, my colleagues and I did a research study[1] to learn about the coping strategies women use to cope with intimate partner violence victimization. I'll share a brief overview of that study here to offer ideas for how you can build and organize your own Coping Toolbox for navigating challenges that arise in your abuse recovery process.

In this study, we learned from existing research, as well as in-depth interviews with ten women who sought help from domestic violence shelters in North Carolina. Using these resources, we developed a framework called the "Coping Window" to organize the methods survivors use to cope with abuse. Although we were focusing primarily on people currently facing abuse, the framework is also useful for understanding coping strategies once the abusive relationship ends. In the Coping Window, the outer window frame represents the unique context surrounding each person's experiences. Contextual factors, such as threats of ongoing abuse, parenting issues, and cultural values, influence how survivors choose to cope within their unique situation.

Inside the Coping Window, there are two axes: The Focus Axis and the Resource Axis. We divided the Focus axis into two categories: emotion-focused and problem-focused coping strategies. This means people can use coping strategies that directly address the problem they're facing, or they can use strategies that aim to help them manage emotional responses to that problem. Along the Resource axis, there also were two categories: intrapersonal and interpersonal. Intrapersonal coping strategies are those people can do on their own, and interpersonal strategies are those that involve looking to others for support. When you put the two axes together, this results in the following four types of coping strategies:

Emotion-Focused/Intrapersonal Coping. With these strategies, people cope by using self-reflection and other personal strategies to manage and work through emotions. Examples included keeping hope, using positive self-talk, turning to spiritual beliefs, and releasing negativity by engaging in activities like hobbies, exercise, or journaling.

Emotion-Focused/Interpersonal Coping. People also may find it helpful to cope with difficult emotions by turning to others for support. This may include reaching out to family and friends for emotional support, as well as by using similar strategies mentioned above (e.g., hobbies and exercise), but doing them with others.

Problem-Focused/Intrapersonal Coping. These strategies involve working on one's own to directly address specific problems. In particular, this may involve making and then implementing active plans for how to address the problem.

Problem-Focused/Interpersonal Coping. This category involves reaching out for help from others for tangible support to address problems. Examples of people and organizations to which people may turn include friends and family, community agencies, crisis lines, law enforcement, and housing agencies.

For the most part, people use a mix of coping strategies when faced with problems, although many people gravitate toward certain coping styles. Personally, my tendency is to lean toward coping with hard times by trying to directly solve or manage the problems I'm facing, and I usually try to do this on my own as much as I can. However, I've learned over time, and especially when dealing with different types of long-term experiences of recovering from past abuse, that sometimes I need to break out of my normal coping strategies because I need different types of support. Sometimes, even if I'd rather try to figure something out on my own, I know I'll get further by talking with a friend or professional to come up with the best plan for addressing the problem. And, even though my preference would always be to get a problem resolved, sometimes I just need to focus on working through my emotions, especially if I'm facing a problem that won't be resolved quickly.

So, let's turn now to thinking through your own Coping Toolbox. I want you to think of two versions of your Coping Toolbox. First, what's currently in your Coping Toolbox? But second, what could you add to your Coping

Toolbox to give you a wider range of options of coping strategies? Complete Exercise 2 to envision these two versions of your Coping Toolbox. After the exercise, we'll talk through the benefits of specific coping strategies that may be especially useful for survivors of abuse, so feel free to return to this exercise as you go through that section to add new tools to your envisioned future toolbox.

Exercise 2: Your Current and Envisioned Future Coping Toolbox

Picture the image of a toolbox. Just like your Trauma Backpack, try to visualize what your Coping Toolbox looks like, including how large it is, what color it is, and how many compartments it has. Again, if it would be helpful to you, consider drawing a picture of your Coping Toolbox on a separate piece of paper.

Next, imagine if we were to open up your Coping Toolbox and find that it's organized similar to the Coping Window framework. With that framework in mind, write a list in each section of this *current* version of your Coping Toolbox to represent the coping strategies you already use:

Your Current Coping Toolbox
_____

Emotion-Focused/Intrapersonal Tools   Emotion-Focused/Interpersonal Tools

Problem-Focused/Intrapersonal Tools   Emotion-Focused/Interpersonal Tools

---

Before you begin planning other tools to add to your Coping Toolbox, look over your current Coping Toolbox. In which areas do you have many coping tools readily available, and in which areas are you lacking? Which coping tools do you usually gravitate toward, and which are more difficult for you?

Now, envision a new and improved version of your Coping Toolbox, in which you've taken time to build additional strategies. Again, you may wish to add to this new and improved version of your Coping Toolbox as you read on and learn more about how the coping strategies listed below can be helpful to survivors of past abuse.

Your Envisioned New and Improved Coping Toolbox

Emotion-Focused/Intrapersonal Tools   Emotion-Focused/Interpersonal Tools

Problem-Focused/Intrapersonal Tools   Emotion-Focused/Interpersonal Tools

Tools for Your Coping Toolbox

As a survivor of abuse, it's wise to pack your toolbox with as many helpful coping strategies as you can. The process of building your Coping Toolbox can be empowering as you reclaim your freedom to make choices for yourself. As we'll touch on often throughout this book, while your partner was abusing you, they likely controlled many of your choices. It's normal in that situation to lose touch with some of your personal preferences. You may feel like you have no idea what would work for you to cope. Be gentle with yourself if you're not even sure where to start with filling in your Coping Toolbox. Try to view the process of building up your coping strategies with a sense of curiosity and a chance to explore your personal preferences. Keep in mind that different coping strategies will resonate with you, so don't worry if something that works well for others doesn't work for you.

The strategies listed below are just a starting point for understanding the coping tools that can be useful for survivors of abuse. Don't put unnecessary pressure on yourself to use coping strategies that don't work for you or aren't practical for you to use. It's wise to try new things a few times before you make a decision if it'll be a good tool to use on a regular basis. Sometimes, it takes time to get over some initial discomfort when you're trying something new. So, for example, let's say you try yoga because you've heard friends talk about how relaxing it is. But when you go to your first yoga class, you find it to be very stressful because you can't figure out the poses and have a hard time quieting your mind. Of course, you can go just that once if you really hate it, but it also may be a good idea to give it a couple more tries to see if you can work through that initial discomfort and start to enjoy it. You also could try using the same strategy in a different way—such as doing a yoga video at home instead of going to a class.

View the process of finding the right coping strategies for you as a big experiment! And, keep in mind it's wise to have different strategies to draw upon in different situations throughout your recovery process. Sometimes, you may need a coping tool to help you release pent up energy—such as an intense workout—but other times it may be helpful to have a strategy focusing on clearing your mind—such as meditation. If you can envision any situations related to your recovery process for which a certain coping tool would be helpful, keep it in mind as part of your Coping Toolbox. Below, you'll find examples of coping strategies that may be especially helpful for survivors in the process of triumphing over abuse.

Counseling

We'll take a closer look at counseling later in this book, but it's important to include counseling here because it can be a powerful coping resource. An appropriately trained professional counselor or therapist can help you process your experiences with abuse and the recovery process. Counseling can serve as both a problem-focused and an emotion-focused coping strategy. Counselors can help you problem-solve when faced with challenges, and they also can help you examine and manage and understand your emotional reactions to difficult situations. Obviously, as a counselor myself, I'm biased in thinking that counseling can be a wonderful coping tool. I've also found my own personal counseling to be instrumental in processing my own experiences with abuse, so I can personally attest to the value of counseling from a client perspective as well.

Of course, there can be significant barriers to accessing counseling, such as financial costs, time needed to go to appointments, and other logistical challenges like transportation or childcare. Increasingly, more domestic violence agencies are helping connect survivors to counseling resources, such as by offering free or low-cost counseling through their agencies or by making referrals to well-trained counselors in their community. If you don't already know how to connect with a counselor in your area, a domestic violence agency may be a good starting point for tracking down a good referral, even if you aren't in immediate danger. Later in this book, we'll cover additional tips for finding a counselor who is competent to serve victims and survivors of abuse. For now, keep in mind that a qualified counselor can be a powerful tool to help you cope with problems and emotions associated with the abuse you've experienced.

Support Groups

Support groups are similar to counseling, in that they can serve as both emotion-focused and problem-focused coping resources. Support groups are more interpersonal in nature, as they involve meeting with others who've faced similar challenges. For many survivors, support groups are a huge source of validation, encouragement, and even friendship. Support groups for survivors of abuse often can be found through domestic violence agencies, women's centers, and faith communities. These groups can be facilitated by professionals (such as a counselor) or peers.

Every support group has its own unique feel, format, and approach, so consider what you'd most like to get out of a support group, and try to find a group that matches your goals. If you're shy, it can feel uncomfortable to go to a support group. However, you should never feel pressured to talk or share more than you're comfortable disclosing. A good support group will provide each person with the time they need to open up about their own experiences if and when they're ready.

One reason support groups can be so valuable for survivors is because isolation is a common tactic used by abusers, so you may find yourself feeling lonely and disconnected from others in the aftermath of abuse. Support groups can help connect you to others who can offer a sense of solidarity and understanding. Fellow support group members also can offer ideas for working through problems, such as how to navigate a custody court case with an abusive partner or how to talk to your children about abuse. Again, however, a good support group will offer suggestions but empower and encourage you to make decisions for yourself.

Online Support and Resources

In-person support groups offer many potential benefits, but there are a lot of great online resources available to add to your Coping Toolbox, either in addition to or instead of face-to-face support groups. These online resources can be especially valuable for people who aren't able to access in-person support groups, such as those in rural areas or people who have disabilities or transportation issues.

We've seen the power of online communities for survivors through our See the Triumph social media campaign. Originally, our goal for building See the Triumph was to share the stories of survivors who had participated in our research. However, as See the Triumph has grown, we've watched it evolve into a supportive online community through which survivors can connect with one another and receive encouragement from the stories and insights we share based on our research. Throughout our time operating See the Triumph, we've learned about and partnered with several other great survivor-led social media campaigns and communities.

One of the great things about social media-based support resources is that they bring the support right to you. For example, if you follow our See the Triumph Facebook page or other similar pages, and especially if you were to set it up so you'd see posts from those pages first in your news feed, then supportive messages and information are delivered to you without much effort on your part. We've heard from several people over the years how much those daily messages were critical to their journey of healing and recovering from past abuse.

Beyond social media, there are other potentially useful coping resources and tools available online. Always be sure to consider the credibility of online information, but you can find many credible, survivor-focused organizations online that offer useful information for different aspects of the recovery process. Of course, it's important to consider safety and privacy issues any time you use online resources, especially if you still face any threat of any type of harm from your abuser. Remember that any information you share in a public online forum could be seen by your abuser. To learn more about ways to promote your safety when using technology, check out some of the resources that the National Network to End Domestic Violence (NNEDV) has created through their Technology Safety project (https://www.techsafety.org/).

In addition, you may find other coping resources online through more general platforms that aren't specific to abuse. For example, many people use meditation apps to help them relax and re-center. Technology is ever-changing, so be on the lookout for new tools and resources that you could add to your Coping Toolkit. To get you started in identifying potentially helpful online coping resources and tools, take time to explore websites, social media campaigns, online communities, and apps that may be helpful to you, and note them in your Coping Toolbox.

Journaling

During an abusive relationship, journaling may not be available as a coping tool because of fear your abuser would find your journal and use its contents against you. However, once you've established safety and privacy, journaling can be a wonderful intrapersonal coping resource. There can be real power when putting pen or pencil to paper (or even typing in an electronic journal) to get thoughts out of your head and written in your journal. Journaling can help you with both emotion-focused and problem-focused coping, as you can process both your feelings and your circumstances in your journal. Journaling offers freedom to write about anything on your mind, and often during the writing process, you gain clarity and insights.

I know some people who write in their journal every single day, and others (myself included!) who use journaling from time to time when needed. The key to using journaling as an effective coping resource is giving yourself permission to use it how you need it. Don't let it create additional stress by becoming an obligation that you feel bad about if you miss a day (or even a few months!) of journaling. You can find many useful journal formats at your local bookstore or online. However, there's nothing wrong with just using an inexpensive note-book or just writing on paper you have on hand. Here are a few specific journa-ling techniques that can be especially useful for survivors of abuse:

Free-form Journaling. This is stream-of-consciousness writing. Just put the pen to the paper and let your thoughts lead you where they want to go. Don't edit yourself or worry about grammar. Don't worry if your thoughts bounce around all over the place, either. Let the words flow from your mind to the paper and see what comes out. Often, when people first start this type of journaling, they feel like their mind is all over the place, but over time their thoughts start to take on a more cohesive form, and greater insights and patterns of thinking start to emerge.

Writing Letters that You Won't Ever Send. This is one of my favorite jour-naling techniques, and it's especially powerful for survivors as they process feelings toward their abusers, as well as others who have hurt them or weren't there for them in the ways they needed them to be. If you feel like you wish you could give your abuser (or other people) a piece of your mind, but you know you can't for a variety of reasons (including your safety), then this type of journaling might be for you. You can start your letter by simply writing, "Dear _____," and go from there. You may find that you write words you'd never say aloud, and your letter may start with a lot of cursing! Whatever comes out in this letter is what you need to get out at the moment you're writing, and because the person you're writing to won't ever see it, you can just say anything on your mind and not worry about how they'll take it.

Often when I've done this type of journaling, I find that my letters start out really angry, and then as I get to the end, I'm writing with more compassion or understanding toward the person, but that's not necessary for this type of journaling to work. This form of journaling also can be useful as an intermediate step before you actually have to communicate with the person you're addressing. For example, imagine that you've gotten an abusive email from your abuser, and you know that what you *want to* say wouldn't be helpful. Before you respond (if any response at all is needed), take time to write an unsendable letter to get your immediate reactions out, and then you can separately write out a more brief, appropriate response. Overall, letter writing journal entries can help you sort through your emotions and conflicts with other people. Remember that although you're writing with the other person in mind, these letters are for you and your own coping and healing.

Art Journaling. Journaling doesn't have to include only written words. By integrating art into your journaling, you bring a different level of creativity to the writing process, as well as allow yourself to express yourself without the constraints of language and words. Art journaling can take many forms, such as doodling, making a collage or vision board, or even drawing comic book-like story lines. Bring your creative mind to this process.

Writing Prompts and Lists. Using writing prompts or lists can add a bit more structure to your journaling and help guide you through different aspects of your healing journey. You can prepare writing prompts that you'd like to cover in your journal ahead of time, such as by brainstorming a list of ideas of topics and questions you'd find helpful. Some examples of writing prompts that may be helpful include the following:

◊   What do I like about myself?

◊   How did my childhood affect my relationship with my abuser?

◊   What are my future goals and dreams for myself?

◊   How were friends and family there for me during my abusive relationship, and how did they let me down?

◊   What do I want to look for in a future romantic partner? How will I know when I'm ready to enter another relationship?

◊   What, if any, red flags did I miss when I first started dating my abusive partner?

◊   My vision for my life ten years from now is….

◊   The ways I've grown stronger through my journey of recovering from abuse include….

◊   Things I've learned about myself through my experience of being abused….

In addition to writing about prompts such as those listed above, some survivors find writing lists in their journals to be helpful, especially as a problem-focused coping strategy. Lists can be a great addition to your journal because they don't require complete sentences or any specific writing structure. Lists can also help you break down problems or goals into specific steps to take. So, for example, you might list out all the current challenges you're facing, as well as the current resources or opportunities you have to address those challenges. You also could make a list of steps to take to resolve a specific problem or move toward a goal. Many challenges faced along the journal of recovering from past abuse can seem overwhelmingly large, so using lists can help you break those challenges down into more manageable pieces and steps.

Overall, journaling has many possible applications in your Coping Toolbox. You may find that journaling is helpful every day or just on certain occasions. Consider which forms of journaling might be useful to you as you think through whether journaling might be a good addition to your Coping Toolbox.

Art and Music

Through our See the Triumph research, we've heard from many survivors that art and music can be powerful tools for coping and healing. In fact, we've even created a *See the Triumph Healing Arts Workshop curriculum* that offers specific arts-based activities for survivors designed to help them process their experiences. You can learn more about this curriculum and request a free copy here: http://www.seethetriumph.org/see-the-triumph-healing-arts-workshops.html.

One of the most powerful aspects of art and music for survivors is that they allow opportunities for coping and growth that are free from pressure to "find the right words" or even translate your experiences and emotions into language. It can be difficult indeed to put into words such complex emotions and experiences related to abuse. By creating your own art or music, or by experiencing art or music created by someone else with similar experiences, you can capture dimensions of your experiences that aren't easily described through written or spoken words. Art and music also tap into your creative side, and creativity offers important benefits for survivors. Engaging in creative activities is a way to learn about yourself as you expand your thinking and step outside of your normal comfort zones. For survivors who've been confined and controlled by their abusers, creative outlets can offer powerful tools for reclaiming parts of themselves from which they've become disconnected, as well as discovering new parts of their identity they've not yet explored.

A lot of people feel uncomfortable engaging in the arts or music if they don't consider themselves to be an "artist" or "musician." I can relate to this, as I am certainly not a skilled artist, and despite many years of piano lessons as a child, my musical talents are pretty much nonexistent! However, the great thing about using art and music as tools for coping and healing is that it's not about the *quality* of the finished product, but rather the benefits of the *process* of the experience. You could paint the ugliest picture in the world, but if the process of making it was useful to you, that's what matters! Or, banging on a drum set might sound like noise pollution to others, but if it provides an emotional release to you, then it's done the trick!

There are many different ways to use art and music as coping tools and as part of your healing journey. A formal route is working with an art therapist or music therapist, who are professionally trained therapists that use art and/or music as part of the counseling process. To find a credentialed art therapist, you can find a database on the Art Therapy Credentials Board website: https://www.atcb.org/. Also, the American Music Therapy Association offers a directory of music therapists through their website: https://www.musictherapy.org/. You also might consider seeking out art classes or music lessons in your community if you're interested in building specific skills.

However, art and music can be just as powerful tools even if just using them on your own. As noted above, this could be as simple as doing doodling in your journal. Consider what other art mediums might be a good fit for you, with anything from adult coloring books to painting to pottery to photography. Explore local art galleries or museums to find inspiration. Just remember that your art doesn't need to look like it belongs in a museum to be valuable to your healing process!

When it comes to music, writing music is one way to use music as a coping tool, but many survivors find it helpful to simply find the right music to listen to at the right time. Keep a list of songs that help you feel empowered or at peace, as well as songs that remind you of your worth. Take some time to set up playlists of songs that inspire you. If your spirituality is important to you,

you might consider songs that speak to your spiritual side. For me personally, music has been an extremely valuable coping tool through some difficult times, and I've had days where I've listened to the same inspirational song over and over again until the positive message really sinks in. And, believe me when I tell you that you wouldn't want to listen to my singing voice, but I can tell you that sometimes, singing (even if badly and off-key) a favorite song out loud can help its message sink in even more than just listening to it!

Exercise

Physical exercise can be a powerful coping strategy. Since exercise can be done on your own or with other people, it can be used as either an interpersonal or intrapersonal coping tool. And, while the physical release can also help you manage your emotions, the mind-clearing benefits can be useful for problem-focused coping as well. Exercising can be a tool that you adapt to a lot of circumstances and make it work for you on many levels.

Exercising has always been one of my personal favorites when it comes to coping techniques. It may not be as appealing to others who don't enjoy exercising as much, but running in particular has been much more than just a way for me to stay in shape. Running has offered countless hours to clear my mind and think through difficult situations in my life. I've had lots of occasions when I've worked through powerful emotions like anger and sadness while running. When I run by myself, I can free my mind to think about whatever I need to ponder at that moment. But I also enjoy running with friends and talking and supporting each other through the challenging situations while we're logging our miles.

Beyond the immediate benefits of running, I've found that I get a lot from the symbolic meanings of running as well. For example, running a longer distance than I've ever run before reminds me I can challenge my limits in other areas of life. And, when I've run races before, training for the race and then finally crossing the finish line reminds me that I can set and achieve goals in all areas of my life. I've run a few marathons and usually am in tears toward the end of the race–and not because of the pain in my legs at the time! The tears have come as I've reflected on how the marathon was symbolic of how I've been pressing through difficult times in my life, and that I can make it to the finish line, no matter how difficult it is.

If all of this sounds great to you, but you hate running with a passion, don't worry because virtually any type of exercise can offer these types of benefits to you. In addition to running, I like a lot of different types of exercise, including hiking, walking, weightlifting, and Zumba classes, and pretty much any type of exercise can be useful for helping to manage emotions and clear your mind, as well as offer opportunities to set goals for yourself and connect with other people. The keys to using exercise as a coping tool are (1) to find types of exercise that you enjoy and (2) to intentionally use your selected types of exercise as part of your Coping Toolbox. Think through exercises that you enjoy, and if you need to, experiment by trying new forms of exercise so you have more options to choose from. When trying new forms of exercise, it's a good idea to give it a few tries before deciding if you like it–sometimes, just the newness of a form of exercise can feel uncomfortable, but if you give it some time to adjust, you may find you like it more than the first try!

Once you've figured out some types of exercise that could work for you, think through specifically when and how they would be useful as a coping strategy. So, for example, if walking is your exercise of choice, consider how you could use it to help cope with different types of challenging situations. Would you prefer to walk alone, or would you rather walk with a friend? You might want to find a friend or two who enjoy walking who'd be up for a walk if you'd like to use that time to get their guidance on a difficult situation you're facing. Think through places you can walk, whether that's in your neighborhood, at a local park, or indoors on a treadmill. By being intentional, planning ahead, and thinking about how you can use your chosen forms of exercise as coping tools, they'll be ready for you to use when you need them.

Yoga

Yoga is a specific form of exercise that can be a powerful coping tool for survivors, but it also can serve as a spiritual or meditative practice, so I'll talk about it separately from other forms of exercise in this section, and we'll cover some additional relaxation and meditative practices in the next section. In fact, it's because yoga combines the benefits of different types of coping practices that it can offer such powerful coping benefits. The physical activity in yoga offers many of the same benefits of exercise, and its meditative and spiritual components helps foster peace of mind and clarity of thinking.

The use of yoga in the recovery process for survivors of intimate partner violence has so many potential applications that researchers have begun to study its benefits. For example, one study[2] published in the journal, *Spirituality in Clinical Practice,* examined the use of yoga as an added component of group therapy for survivors, and they found some of the potential benefits included greater self-confidence, healing, and more connection between the mind and body. In another study[3] from the *Counseling Outcome Research and Evaluation* journal, researchers found that adult female survivors who participated in a trauma-sensitive yoga program for eight weeks described benefits to their physical, emotional, and spiritual health.

Yoga is primarily an emotion-focused coping strategy, although the mental calmness it provides, along with the time and opportunity for self-reflection, can offer benefits for problem-solving as well. Yoga can be an intrapersonal practice, such as if you practice or attend a class on your own. However, you also can attend yoga classes to meet or attend with others for additional interpersonal social support. Yoga has grown in popularity in the past few decades, so classes can be found in many different settings, including gyms, community centers, and even libraries. Most places that offer classes provide a description of the specific type of yoga classes they offer, which is important to consider since some classes are more relaxation-based, while others (such as hot yoga) are more rigorous. In addition to general yoga classes, there's a growing number of specific Trauma-Sensitive Yoga practitioners, which is a model developed at the Center for Trauma and Embodiment at the Justice Resource Institute in Brookline, Massachusetts. To learn more about Trauma-Sensitive Yoga and find a trained facilitator, visit the Center's website at https://www.traumasensitiveyoga.com/.

Relaxation and Meditative Practices

In addition to yoga, many other types of relaxation and meditative practices may be useful coping tools for survivors. Greater relaxation and mindfulness can be valuable for coping with difficult emotions, as well as for gaining clarity to help work through problems that arise. These practices can be done on your own, with other people, or through formal classes and group training programs. Some relaxation practices can be done in even just a few minutes, so they can be useful for navigating stressful situations in the moment. Below, I'll describe two examples of relaxation strategies that may be useful to consider adding to your Coping Toolbox: relaxation breathing and mindfulness.

> *Relaxation Breathing.* This is one of the simplest relaxation strategies to use, but it can be difficult to put into practice in a high-stress, busy moments of life. Learning to focus on and slow down your breathing can help you along your journey to triumph over abuse. Of course, you'll likely deal with a lot of situations that require a lot more than a pause and a deep breath to make your way through. However, the

simplicity of relaxation breathing allows you to use this tool anytime, anywhere, or in any situation. Start practicing by taking some time to just sit or lie down in a quiet place, and then turn your attention to your breath. Begin to slow down the rate of your inhalation and exhalation. It may help to focus on a specific number of seconds per breath (such as five seconds per inhale or exhale), but this isn't necessary if it feels more stressful to you to have set rules. But that's basically all there is to it! Don't let the simplicity of relaxation breathing fool you, though. It's a powerful tool, whether you use it for ten seconds or a lot longer. And, the more you practice relaxation breathing, the easier it will be to use it in higher-stress situations when it can help you calm your emotions and be ready to face the challenges coming your way.

Mindfulness. Practicing mindfulness means learning to pay attention to what you are experiencing. In our technology-driven, busy world today, this is often much more difficult than it sounds! There are so many distractions that keep us from paying full attention to where we are, who we're with, what we're doing, and what we're feeling. Developing a mindfulness practice helps you learn to tune into these experiences so you become more fully engaged with your senses and emotions. There are formal approaches to learning mindfulness, such as Mindfulness-Based Stress Reduction (which you can learn about through the Center for Mindfulness at the University of Massachusetts Medical School here: https://www.umassmed.edu/cfm/mindfulness-based-programs/). However, it's also possible to learn mindfulness on your own just by simply practicing it. For example, the next time you're eating a meal, try slowing down and focusing on the tastes, smell, feel, and look of the food while you're eating it. Or, the next time you're taking a walk, turn off your music and try just looking at the scenery around you, listening to the noises you hear, and feeling the temperature of the air on your skin.

Although mindfulness seems very simple, it can have powerful coping benefits. One of the most significant possible benefits for survivors is by helping them to be more mindful and attentive to their emotions. While being abused, survivors often disconnect from their feelings so they can make it through the stress and crisis of the immediate situation. However, over the long-term, this pattern of disconnecting can lead you to avoid paying attention to your feelings, thoughts, and needs. For that reason, mindfulness is an especially helpful tool for survivors. As an added benefit, although mindfulness certainly can be combined with other forms of meditation and relaxation, there's no requirement that you have to sit still and try and calm your mind, which can be intimidating and uncomfortable for many people.

Overall, learning to relax and become more mindful are important steps on the journey of recovering from past abuse. You may feel silly if it's difficult for you to relax—after all, shouldn't relaxation not add stress to your life? But, the things that survivors carry in their Trauma Backpacks can make it difficult to relax, so know that if you have a hard time relaxing, then you're not alone! Personally, this has been a really challenging thing for me to learn—I'm a high-energy person who has a hard time sitting still, so relaxation and mindfulness don't come naturally to me. However, taking time to learn how to regulate your emotions and thoughts through these practices is well worth it, and they can become important resources to draw upon throughout the abuse recovery process.

Spiritual and Religious Practices and Beliefs

Everyone has a unique belief system, so it'd be impossible to give one overarching description of the ways spiritual and religious practices and beliefs can become coping resources along the journey of recovering from abuse. However, because these practices and beliefs can be such a personal and significant part of people's lives, it's important to consider whether and how these are important to add to your personal Coping Toolbox.

I'll share a bit of personal experience here as an example of how my spirituality helps me when it comes to coping. Speaking from my perspective as a person of faith (I am a Christian), I can tell you that my belief in a higher power was crucial to surviving and recovering from abuse. I found great comfort in reading scripture, listening to sermons and worship music, and connecting with others in my church. Sometimes, when my circumstances were just not making any sense, I was able to cope because I relied on my faith and believed things would work out, even if I couldn't see the positive ending at the current moment. My faith helped me make it through difficult times, as I could remind myself that there was something bigger than me guiding me through my current challenges.

Although my religious perspective is the Christian faith, I believe many other faith backgrounds can offer comfort, peace, and strength while coping with abuse and its aftermath. I encourage you to reflect on your own belief system and how you can put your beliefs into practice to support your coping efforts. You don't have to ascribe to any particular faith tradition or religion, or even believe in God, to be able to draw upon spiritual resources for coping. Start with whatever spirituality means to you right now, and draw from that meaning to help you cope and make meaning of your circumstances.

I'll add a brief note of caution about spirituality and religion, as these may be areas that were linked to your abuse if your abuser used your beliefs to hurt you, and some survivors experience stigma and hurt from others in their spiritual communities that causes added hurt. Through our See the Triumph research, we heard these themes from many survivors, and you can read about some of this research in our See the Triumph Collection on the topic of "Addressing the Stigma Surrounding Intimate Partner Violence in Churches" (http://www.seethetriumph.org/collection-addressing-the-stigma-surrounding-intimate-partner-violence-in-churches). If you experienced spiritual abuse or if you faced hurt within your spiritual community, it may be difficult to rely on your spiritual beliefs or practices as coping strategies. You may find it helpful to use other strategies to help you cope with your feelings as you work through those hurts. And, your recovery process can offer an opportunity to reevaluate your spiritual and religious beliefs independent from your abuser and others who may have hurt you.

Spending Time in Nature

One time, I was counseling a client who was involved at the time in a very dangerous abusive relationship. Her abuser was in prison at the time, so there was no risk that he would be stalking or following her during the time we worked together. At the time, I was working in a tiny, dark office—a little larger than a closet! I was fortunate that there was a nice park right behind my offices, so once I knew clients well and if they agreed to it, sometimes we'd move our sessions outdoors, either to a bench or by taking a walk around the park. For this particular client, the contrast between my confining office and the park became a powerful metaphor for how she felt in the relationship. One day, we walked from my office to the middle of the open field in the park, and she shared how it felt so freeing in the field compared to the office, much like she felt confined in her relationship.

Since that time, I've always reflected on how powerful natural environments can be for survivors. Being outside is one of my personal favorite coping strategies, as it helps me unplug from the distractions of technology, clear my mind, and relieve stress. As with any coping strategy, this one may not be a good fit for you. But, if you enjoy the outdoors, give some thought to how time in nature might be a good addition to your Coping Toolbox.

You don't have to be an avid outdoors-person to reap the benefits of spending time in nature. Even just getting some fresh air by taking a quick walk around your neighborhood or a local park can offer benefits. However, if you're like me, I've found that the deeper I get into nature, the more mind-clearing benefits I experience. Of course, it's important to be safe, so for most of us, it's wise to find a friend or a group to explore nature with, whether through hiking, paddling, biking, or any number of other nature-based activities. While nature can certainly be enjoyed on your own, it also can provide opportunities for deep conversations with others, which again can help you work through emotions and problems.

Outdoor adventures also can serve as symbolic metaphors for certain aspects of the recovery journey. Just try hiking to the top of a mountain and see if you don't feel like a conqueror! Learning new outdoor skills or trying something that is outside your comfort zone can help you see that you can gain new knowledge and skills and overcome fears in other areas of your life. I'll never forget the first time I tried standup paddleboarding. I was intimidated and scared because it looked so hard, but then I tried it and loved it! And, learning to balance on the paddleboard gave me food for thought about learning to feel more balanced in other areas of life.

Creating a Personal Safe Space

A few years ago, there was a lifestyle and home decorating trend called *hygge* that started gaining popularity in the United States. It came from a Danish concept that roughly means being comfortable and cozy. Think of snuggling under a cozy blanket on a soft couch or getting a cup of coffee while catching up with a close friend. When I first heard this term, I loved it and knew I wanted more hygge in my life! I think this concept can be meaningful for survivors because many survivors, especially if they lived with their abusers, are used to feeling anything but comfortable and cozy in their living environments.

You don't have to embrace the hygge lifestyle—or even understand it—to consider creating some sort of personal safe space as part of your overall Coping Toolkit plans. A safe space could be a specific area or chair in your home, or it may be an item or two (such as a cozy blanket or a favorite coffee mug) that you can take with you to help bring a feeling of comfort and safety with you to different spaces. A personal safe space is sort of like a grown-up version of a "time out corner" for little children whose parents send them there to calm down and regroup when their emotions or behavior get out of control. However, your safe space shouldn't feel like punishment, but rather like a reward or special treat. Designating your personal safe space can also provide you with a comfortable environment for practicing some of the other coping strategies we've discussed, such as journaling, relaxation breathing, and mindfulness meditation. As you're reclaiming many different aspects of yourself while recovering from abuse, consider how reclaiming physical spaces as your own can help you feel worthy of care, comfort, safety, and support.

Other Self-Care Practices that Work for You

The coping strategies listed in this section offer you a starting point for considering which tools to include in your Coping Toolbox. That said, we all have unique preferences and resources available to help us cope, so the most important factor is considering what works best for you to cope in healthy, adaptive ways. There are many other self-care practices that could help you cope. Don't be afraid to add uniquely-you self-care strategies to your Coping Toolbox. Maybe you have a favorite hobby to add to the list, you enjoy baking cookies when you're feeling stressed, or even enjoy going for long, relaxing drives on a weekend afternoon to clear your mind. If a strategy works for you and doesn't create additional problems in your life (like financial stress), then include it in your personal Coping Toolbox. This is *your* set of coping resources, and you want it to reflect your preferences. The key is to build a set of tools that you can and will use when you face challenging circumstances or difficult emotions. Your Coping Toolbox doesn't have to look like anyone else's, and in fact, the more specialized it is to your preferences, the more likely you'll be able to put it to good use when needed.

Conclusion

Throughout your journey of triumphing over abuse, and really for the rest of your life, it's important to take care of yourself and make your wellbeing a priority. This can be more complicated than it sounds for survivors, because it's natural to carry the effects of trauma around, as we discussed with the Trauma Backpack metaphor. You can lighten the load of the Trauma Backpack by working through the trauma. However, this requires a well-built Coping Toolbox to ensure you have the coping resources and self-care practices in place to navigate the complex problems and emotions that arise while processing and moving beyond past abuse.

In this chapter, we've talked through the process of building your Coping Toolbox to ensure you're in the best position to navigate the challenging topics we'll cover in the chapters ahead. Before you move on to the rest of the chapters, I invite you to pause so you can take a look at your current Coping

Toolbox. Consider if you have enough coping tools at your disposal to be ready to start working through the more emotionally intense topics in the chapters that follow. Even in the very next chapter, when we'll talk about surrounding yourself with the right types of social support, we'll cover difficult topics, like working through hurts from friends and family who didn't provide the support you needed while you were in an abusive relationship or after it ended. If you're just starting to build up your coping resources, it's okay to take a pause from reading this book and set it aside to come back to once you've got a solid set of coping strategies in place.

If you continue reading now, you may want to bookmark or dog-ear this chapter so you can return to it if and when difficult emotions or experiences come up as you read. For example, if reading about child custody issues begins to trigger stress because you relate to those challenges, come back to this chapter and your Coping Toolbox to be reminded of positive coping tools to help manage those emotions, such as journaling, talking to a counselor, or going for a run.

As someone who faced abuse, you may be used to operating in "Survival Mode" and powering through difficult experiences and emotions in order to make it through to another day. Survival Mode is a necessary way to operate during times of extreme duress, but eventually operating in this way can take a toll on your mind, body, and emotions. Learning to live in a peaceful, nonviolent way means re-adjusting to a new life outside of Survival Mode and putting into practice new, sustainable ways of navigating challenges in life. Remember: It's not a sprint to get to the end of the healing and recovery process from past abuse. Take the time you need to work through difficult problems and emotions that arise, and treat yourself well along the way.

References

1. Smith, P. H., Murray, C. E., & Coker, A. (2010). The Coping Window: A contextual framework for understanding the methods women use to cope with battering. *Violence and Victims, 25*, 18–28.
2. Nguyen-Feng, V., Morrissette, J., Lewis-Dmello, A., Michel, H., Anders, D., Wagner, C., & Clark, C. J. (2019). Trauma-sensitive yoga as an adjunctive mental health treatment for survivors of intimate partner violence: A qualitative examination. *Spirituality in Clinical Practice, 6*, 27–43. DOI:10.1037/scp0000177
3. Ong, I., Cashwell, C. S., & Downs, H. A. (2019). Trauma-sensitive yoga: A collective case study of women's trauma recovery from intimate partner violence. *Counseling Outcome Research and Evaluation, 10*, 19–33. DOI:10.1080/21501378.2018.1521698

3

SURROUNDING YOURSELF WITH THE RIGHT SUPPORT

"Many people who know me still don't know that I've been abused, but I'm freer to talk about it, able to be my own woman. I set boundaries with others now and am aware of abuse in the early stages so I can release anyone with whom I cannot be on equal terms. I tend not to waste my time or anger on friends or dates who exhibit this behavior, but to just state what I need and let them be wherever they are, and move on if it is not workable. For a long time, I would feel a lot of resentment at being treated badly. Now I mostly focus on finding people who have integrity and know how to show respect."

~ Domestic Violence Survivor

It just so happens that I started writing this chapter while the United States and the world were in the middle of the coronavirus pandemic. During the pandemic, news stories were coming out almost daily about how the pandemic—and the associated mandates for social distancing and stay-at-home orders—were leading to an increased risk for domestic violence. What explains this link between a virus and domestic violence? Along with all the added stressors everyone was facing at the time—including job losses, economic stress, and uncertainty about how long the pandemic would last—isolation was the key factor.

Most survivors are very familiar with feelings and experiences of isolation. Isolation is a common tactic used by abusers, as well as a potential risk factor for and consequence of intimate partner violence. The requirement for people to be apart from natural support systems during the coronavirus pandemic brought to light the dangers of isolation for victims of domestic violence. But isolation can be just as dangerous at any time, not just during a global pandemic.

Abusers often isolate their partners as one strategy for entrapping them in the relationship. By cutting off their partner's access to friends and family, an abuser can make it less likely that their partner will reach out for help. In addition, by isolating their partners, abusers reduce the chance that a friend, coworker, or neighbor might recognize the abuse is happening. If and when a survivor is finally ready to leave their abusive partner, it's normal for them to look up and realize they've been totally cut off from friends and family, and the prospect of facing the end and the aftermath of the relationship alone can be very daunting.

Isolation—whether actually *being* distant from others or *feeling* loneliness and separation from others—also can be a common challenge for survivors throughout the recovery process. Even when survivors start building a social support network around them—such as with helping professionals or a support group—it's normal to have moments of feeling isolated and alone at different points in the healing journey. After all, the journey to recovering from abuse can be a long, emotional process, and it's natural to feel like others don't fully understand what you're facing.

The dangers of isolation highlight just how critical social support is for survivors. But, it's important to have the right kind of social support surrounding you during the recovery process. Unfortunately, not everybody will be able to provide you with the support you need during this process. Some people will intentionally choose not to support you, and others may unintentionally hurt you or hinder your progress. As such, it's essential to be proactive in two ways to surround yourself with the right support: (1) building and growing connections with the right kind of support and (2) avoiding or setting boundaries with people who could hurt you. This chapter offers considerations for both areas. We begin by looking at how to handle people who've hurt you (intentionally or unintentionally), and then we turn our attention to ways to connect with the right kinds of people to stand by your side during your journey toward triumphing over past abuse.

Overcoming and Preventing Hurts from Others

When you've been abused, you know you've been hurt by your abuser. The hurt they caused you is likely deep, since you trusted them and had loving feelings toward them. It takes time and effort to work through the hurts your abuser caused, and that's the focus of most of the rest of this book. However, sometimes in connection with an abusive relationship, there are other people who hurt you along the way, and these hurts also require their own healing process. Sometimes, hurts from others can feel even more confusing than the direct hurt by your abuser, especially if they were people you turned to for support and they just weren't there for you in the way you needed them to be.

We've heard a lot about hurtful experiences from others in our research[1] on the stigma surrounding intimate partner violence. Survivors have shared how they faced stigmatizing reactions from loved ones, as well as from professionals from whom they sought help. Common stigmatizing responses include victim-blaming, isolation, separation, negative emotions, and loss of status. Our research shows that these responses can be internalized, such as when survivors view themselves as being to blame for their abuse, but they also occur through interactions with others, including the perpetrator and others. Here are a few examples from one of our research studies[2] of the ways that survivors told us they experienced stigma from others:

> "People blamed me for the violence."
> "The friends we had together dropped me when I got divorced."
> "No one will talk to me anymore. I assume he's spread rumors."
> "When I came out about the relationship initially, it was met with disdain and not really acknowledged."
> "I was always labeled as an outcast."
> "I was labeled as a 'loser' or 'pathetic' because I would not fight back with my partner."

Do any of those statements feel familiar to you? I always feel so much sadness when I read statements like that, not only because I can relate to having some similar experiences personally, but also because it seems so unjust that people who've survived the harrowing experiences of abuse would also have to face such negative reactions from others. Knowing how deeply these stigmatizing experiences can cause added stress for survivors, I urge you to be intentional about working toward healing from them. Below, I suggest a 6-step process for working through these hurts. As with all aspects of the healing process, these steps don't necessarily happen in a neat, orderly fashion, but I've pre-sented them in a sequence below to give a sense of what this process can look like. Before moving into these steps, remember to build your coping resources to help manage difficult emotions that might arise along the way.

Step 1: Acknowledge Which Experiences Were Hurtful to You

When you were in survival mode in the immediate crisis of abuse and during the relationship's ending, you might have brushed aside hurtful words and behaviors by others. More pressing needs probably demanded your attention, so it's understandable to have let certain comments or actions slide by in the moment. Or, perhaps you let some people's words or reactions slide because you felt guilty about being upset with them if they were trying to help you. It's also possible that you just didn't have the emotional or physical energy to address those hurts at the time.

I can relate to all of these reasons for not immediately addressing hurtful things I faced from a few people in my life in the aftermath of my abusive rela-tionship. This isn't to say I didn't feel their sting when they happened! I can think back on a few experiences that really hurt at the time, and in some cases I tried (unsuccessfully) to address them with the person when they happened. But, I had more immediate safety and emotional issues to focus on at that time, so I had to set those experiences to the side. This meant that, once the dust settled, I was left with lingering feelings of hurt and confusion about those experiences that I had to work through, in addition to healing from the hurt from my abuser.

As a first step in working through these types of hurtful experiences, reflect on and acknowledge the experiences you had with others that were hurtful to you. It may help to make a list, especially if you can think of a number of hurtful experiences you faced. At this point, don't judge whether you might have "overreacted" or misinterpreted the other person's response. Include hurts that occurred while you were still in the relationship, during the time when the relationship was ending, and other experiences you've faced since then. Think through different types of people you encountered along the way—such as your friends, family, neighbors, fellow church members, and professional helpers, to name just a few. Hopefully, you can also think of ways people in those categories helped you, but for now, focus on the hurts so you can begin to work through them.

Also, be inclusive of things that hurt a lot, as well as those things that may have just stung a little. Remember: Hurt is hurt. Sometimes pain from something you might consider to be a relatively minor issue can grow into a larger pain if you don't process those emotions in a healthy way. Think back to the Trauma Backpack idea, and keep in mind that unprocessed hurts by others—not just your abuser—can become weights you could carry with you into your future.

If you decide to write a list, include the person and what specifically they did that hurt you. For example, one survivor's list might look like the following:

- My sister told me it was my fault because I stayed in the relationship so long.
- The first counselor I went to had a look of horror and judgment when I first told her about the abuse.
- My ex's lawyer treated me like I was stupid, crazy, and making the abuse up.
- Some of the PTA moms wouldn't even look at me in the hallway after we first announced our divorce.

How you set up your list is up to you. You might organize it like a timeline, or you might even consider ranking them in terms of how much hurt each incident caused (e.g., big hurt, medium hurt, or little hurt). Writing this list can be painful as you remember those hurtful experiences, but it also can be a cathartic first step toward developing greater self-compassion. Keep reminding yourself that, just like you didn't deserve any of the abuse by your partner, you also did not deserve to experience hurt by others. Let yourself feel any emotions that come up as you look back on those experiences. Feeling and processing those emotions can be an important part of the healing process.

Some people have a long, painful list of many deeply hurtful experiences, whereas others just experienced a few hurts that didn't have too much of an impact. In fact, it's possible some people won't have had any hurtful experiences by others, and if this applies to you, then you may still find the remaining steps in the process described below helpful to prepare for the possibility of future hurts that may come up during your healing process.

Step 2: Consider What About Each Experience Was Most Hurtful

For the remaining steps, it's wise to focus on one specific hurtful experience or relationship at a time and work through each step, and then come back to Step 2 when you're ready to address the next one. Once you've identified the hurtful experiences that you faced, it's time to start thinking through each one, processing the emotions and thoughts you have related to them, and deciding what, if any, steps you may want to take to address them.

There's really not a right or wrong place to start. You might want to start with a more minor hurt as a way to "warm up" to working through some of the more significant hurts. Or, you might start with the biggest hurts so you can address the ones impacting you the most. You also might decide which hurts to work through first based on what kind of continued relationship or interactions you'll have with each person. For example, if you had a hurtful experience with a professional that you're not likely to meet ever again, you may decide to hold off on processing that hurt while you work through a hurtful experience with a close family member who you see on a regular basis. Start in the place that makes sense to you, and go from there as you feel ready to move forward to other hurtful experiences.

For the specific hurtful experience you've chosen to address now, reflect on why specifically this experience was painful to you. You could write about this in a journal, talk with a counselor or supportive friend, or spend some time in quiet reflection. Identify the specific emotions that come up for you, as well as the reasons you felt so hurt. To help make this and the following steps more concrete, we'll use two statements on the list in Step 1 as examples of how you can apply the action steps. See below for how those statements could be expanded while the survivor explores why they were so hurtful:

- Example 1: "My sister told me it was my fault because I stayed in the relationship so long. This hurt me because I felt like she wasn't understanding how seriously I took my boyfriend's threats that he'd hurt me if I left him. I also felt so sad because my sister has always been so close and supportive to me, and it felt like a betrayal that she was saying it was my fault. I also felt ashamed because her comments made me question my choices, even though I know I made the right choices for me."
- Example 2: "My ex's lawyer treated me like I was stupid, crazy, and making the abuse up. This was hurtful because I felt like my ex was paying the lawyer to rip me apart. It also made me angry because I know the abuse was real, and I know my ex is the one with the problem. This experience also hurt me because it made me feel like I had to defend myself against lies in an environment (the court) where people wouldn't understand what I'd been through."

These examples are just brief illustrations to give you an idea of what the thoughts and feelings associated with these hurts might be. In reality, it's possible it could take pages to fully explore the hurtful aspects of these experiences. Some questions to ask as you process similar hurtful elements are (1) What did I feel?; (2) What did I think?; and (3) What fears did this bring up for me?

As you continue to work through multiple hurts in this process, you may find it helpful to look for themes that come up across different people and experiences. This might offer clues into broader areas for you to focus in your healing journey. For example, if you notice a common theme across multiple people and experiences is that you felt hurt when your voice wasn't heard or your feelings weren't considered, you may one day decide to work on speaking more assertively or expressing your feelings with greater depth. These themes also offer insights into characteristics you'll want to look for in people as you work on building the right types of support, such as people who are interested in really getting to know you and those who take your feelings into consideration.

Step 3: Try to Understand the Motivation(s) Behind People's Hurtful Words or Actions

I'll start this section by saying that, unless you choose to actually talk with people who have hurt you, this step is speculative in nature. And, even if you actually do talk with people who have hurt you, it's possible you won't get accurate or complete answers to the question of why they hurt you. So, this step is one to be taken with an ounce of healthy skepticism. However, there can be value in exploring the actual or possible motivations behind people's hurtful words or actions in the process of working through those hurts.

Understanding motivations can help you gain empathy and possibly make it easier for you to rebuild a relationship with them (if that's appropriate, and we'll discuss that piece further in the next step). Relatedly, gaining insights into the other person's motivations can help you decide what future boundaries you may want to put into place with them, which we'll also discuss in a few moments. In addition, exploring possible motivations can help you in your own emotional and cognitive processing of the hurtful experiences.

Any number of possible motivations could be behind the other person's hurtful words or actions, but below are some common ones:

- Some people don't understand the dynamics of abusive relationships.
- Some people hold stereotypical or biased views that cloud their ability to offer support.

- Some people just aren't the best at offering support to others going through hard times.
- Some people have been manipulated by the abuser to believe bad things about you.
- Some people actually are purposefully and intentionally trying to hurt you.

I believe the vast majority of people who act in hurtful ways toward people who have been abused fall into one or more of the first four categories on this list. I wish that I could tell you that nobody would fall into the final category, but unfortunately, there are people in the world who are mean and negative. And, in the case of domestic violence, there even may be people who are being paid to paint you in a negative light, such as in the example of a former abuser's lawyer trying to damage a survivor's credibility by depicting them as crazy.

If it's not obvious to you what motivation was behind someone's hurtful behavior, consider if that person would be open and safe to have a conversation about this. If this sort of conversation wouldn't be safe or practical, then another way to try and decipher this person's motivations is to reflect on your past experiences with them. Going back to our other example of the survivor's sister saying the abuse was chosen as a result of staying in the relationship, it's possible considering past interactions with the sister will offer insights. For example, this sister may have limited education about abusive relationships, combined with no personal experience with abuse among herself or her friends.

Understanding a person's motivations behind their hurtful words or actions doesn't take the pain away or excuse their hurtful choices. However, this understanding can be immensely helpful as you move onto Step 4.

Step 4: Decide Whether and How to Address Your Hurts with the People Involved

This is a point where things can get really tricky, which is why it's important to consider each person and relationship individually to decide whether and how to address the hurts with them. There will be some people with whom you simply won't have any opportunity to address hurts, such as a lawyer representing your abuser or if someone hurt you and you don't know who they are (e.g., if a law enforcement officer was dismissive or rude to you, but you never got their name). In those cases, you'll necessarily have to address those hurts on your own or with the help of a trusted friend or professional helper. Intentionally honoring and processing your emotions is important for all of these hurts, but especially in cases where there is no option of directly addressing the hurt with the person who hurt you. You may find it helpful to write a letter directed to that person, knowing you'll never send it, but writing it to express your thoughts and feelings in a way that is helpful to you.

Of course, there are other people who hurt you with whom you theoretically could address those hurts directly, but doing so might not be the safest or wisest decision. Therefore, before deciding *how* to address someone about how they hurt you, it's best to start by deciding *whether* this is a good idea in the first place. Consider what you think or know about their motivations as you make this decision. Here are a few other questions to help you decide:

- *Would this person be open to listening and trying to understand your feelings and experiences?* If they'd be likely to keep an open mind and support you, then a direct conversation may prove useful. However, if they're set in their ways or generally lack empathy for others, you may end up feeling like you're talking to a brick wall.
- *Do you want or have to have any sort of future relationship with this person?* If you want or need to have some level of contact with this person in the future, it may be helpful to talk things through, even if just to set some boundaries for your future interactions.
- *Would it be healing or therapeutic for you to address this with them?* Sometimes, talking things through with the other person can be empowering for you as you reclaim your voice and learn to stand up for your wellbeing in relation to others. These conversations also can help bring closure to certain aspects of your healing process.
- *Will you be able to cope with however the other person responds to the conversation?* Unfortunately, you can't guarantee a conversation in which you share your thoughts and feelings will be received in a positive manner. In fact, knowing this person has hurt you in the past means there's a chance they'll hurt you again. Consider whether you're ready to face whatever response they have to the conversation. It might be the case that you're just not ready to risk another experience of getting hurt, so you decide not to address the hurt with them directly now or ever. On the other hand, if you've built strong coping resources and other, positive social support, you may be ready to move forward with addressing this person and be prepared to handle any outcome.

I'll share a personal example of how I thought through—and eventually addressed—concerns about having been hurt by someone in the aftermath of my own past abusive relationship. When that relationship was ending, my abuser told me a professional he'd talked with—but who we both knew—told him I wasn't justified in ending the relationship. I didn't take that secondhand advice at the time, but I was upset that this professional had supposedly given my abuser that guidance, which ultimately could have kept me in an unsafe relationship for a longer time. I was angry, but right as the relationship was ending, I had many other more critical issues I was working through, especially related directly to my abuser. So, I set aside my feelings about this professional for almost a year while I worked through more immediate concerns.

It took time to decide whether to schedule a meeting with this professional. By the time I was ready to address this hurt, I realized I didn't necessarily have to say anything to this professional, as most of my feelings had dissipated by that time. However, I felt concerned that failing to say anything might mean that this professional would give the same misguided advice to someone else, so I decided to schedule a meeting in hopes of educating him about abuse and suggesting he take another approach if a similar issue came up with another couple in the future.

I was very nervous to meet with this professional, but I was pleased to find he was receptive to what I had to say. I felt empowered by the opportunity to give him feedback about how to work more effectively with people impacted by abuse. Even more importantly, there was an added benefit for my healing when I learned that the way that my abuser presented this professional's advice wasn't even what the professional said in the first place. My abuser had misrepresented what the professional said in another attempt to manipulate me. Through this conversation with the professional, I was able to have closure in my feelings about the supposed advice he gave my abuser, and I also gained new insights into the extent of my abuser's manipulation.

Approaches for Addressing Hurtful Experiences

I wish there was a simple decision tree I could offer you to choose how to address hurts by others, but I think it's more useful to share a number of ideas to encourage you to map out the best plan for yourself, keeping in mind that a combination of multiple approaches might have the greatest impact. Below are a few ideas to get you started:

Invite a Conversation

Ask the person if you can talk. If you have the chance for a conversation, explain your feelings and the impact that their words or actions had on you.

Give them a chance to hear your perspective and learn how they can better support you. If the other person is open to hearing you, this conversation may open the door for you to have an even closer, more supportive relationship. You may even find the person didn't realize the harmful impact of their actions. On the other hand, if the other person seems unreceptive to your perspective, be prepared to change the subject or end the conversation so you don't experience further harm.

Write Them a Letter or Email

You may write a letter that you never end up sending, as discussed in Chapter 2. But, you also may find that a written letter can provide an opportunity to share your thoughts and feelings with the other person in a format that offers you time and space to choose the best wording to get your main points across. It's usually ideal to address emotional topics through in-person conversations, but if written communication seems more helpful to you, then trust your instincts.

Adjust the Nature of Your Relationship so that It Feels as Comfortable to You as Possible

We'll talk more about this in the next step on setting healthy boundaries, but for now consider that addressing the hurt you've faced may mean adjusting how you relate to the other person to protect yourself from future hurt and give yourself space during your healing process. This may mean taking a pause from spending time with this person in hopes of rebuilding a closer relationship later, or it may mean permanently distancing yourself from them in a way that helps you keep emotional distance from them. As such, this approach might be a temporary solution until you feel ready for a more in-depth discussion, or it may be a permanent reset of the relationship.

Go No-contact

Some relationships—both romantic and otherwise—simply are unable to be safe, whether physically or emotionally. If possible, if someone who hurt you seems unwilling to commit to a healthier relationship moving forward, you may choose to discontinue the relationship. This could apply to a professional relationship—such as a counselor whose reactions hurt you—or a personal relationship—such as a friendship that needs to end. Ending relationships can be complicated when they're with someone with whom you have to have contact (e.g., a family member or coworker), but the points discussed in the next step of setting healthy boundaries may be helpful for navigating these complicated relationships.

Let's take a look at how this step might apply to our example of the survivor's sister who blamed her for the abuse because she stayed in the relationship. If the survivor decided to attempt a conversation with her sister, she might find her sister is somewhat receptive and apologetic, but still seems to look down on her for having gotten involved with the abusive partner. Since this survivor knows she'll see her sister at extended family events, she might decide to put some emotional distance between them, at least for the time being, to try and prevent additional hurtful interactions, but also keep the door open for a closer relationship later on.

Overall, trust your instincts to guide you about making decisions about the best ways to handle addressing hurts with others, as well as whether you want to address those concerns directly with them at all. Addressing these hurts can be difficult, but as you work through them, it's likely you'll find you're continuing to take important steps forward in your healing journey.

Step 5: Set Healthy Boundaries with Others

If you've survived an abusive relationship, it's likely healthy boundaries are a complicated aspect of relationships for you. Abusers typically have little to no regard for their partners' thoughts, feelings, and boundaries, so part of overcoming an abusive relationship is learning to set and maintain healthy boundaries in relationships. Setting boundaries also is an important step toward building a positive support network, so we'll address this topic again in the latter half of this chapter.

Think of boundaries as a shield from future hurts by people who've been known to hurt you in the past. Set in place protective strategies to minimize those people's opportunities for inflicting more pain. Healthy boundaries offer you greater peace if you decide to allow the possibility of rebuilding a closer relationship if the other person is committed to working on the relationship. Healthy boundaries are about making efforts to both keep bad things out and let good things in.

Healthy boundaries look different for every relationship, but examples of boundaries that may be useful with someone who hurt you include the following:

• Not sharing too many personal details about your life with them until trust is rebuilt

- When you do share personal information with them, doing so gradually so you can stop sharing if you become uncomfortable
- Not spending time alone with them until you've established safety
- Limiting the time you spend communicating with them
- Planning ahead for how to respond if they say or do something else that is hurtful

To further explain what healthy boundaries look like, let's go back to our examples of the former abuser's attorney and the survivor's sister who blamed the survivor for the abuse. For the attorney, the main opportunity this attorney could have to inflict further harm could be in a future court appearance. If that happens, boundaries that might be put in place include asking the survivor's attorney to address inaccurate information more directly, bringing a trusted friend to the courtroom for support, and mentally reminding oneself while the attorney is speaking that just because the attorney is saying something, it doesn't mean it's true or that other people will believe the lies. In the case of the survivor's sister, some useful boundaries might include not sharing too many personal details with the sister until they've rebuilt trust, asking another family member to help make sure they aren't alone in the same room at family gatherings, and having more limited communication with the sister, either temporarily or permanently.

Overall, healthy boundaries serve an important protective role for navigating future interactions and relationships with people who've hurt you in the past. Keep in mind these boundaries may need to be adjusted over time as people show themselves to be more or less trustworthy.

Step 6: Decide Whether to Work Toward Forgiveness

This final step involves considering what sort of closure you want to work toward with respect to hurts you've experienced. You may have heard the saying, "Withholding forgiveness is like drinking poison and expecting the other person to die." There are a lot of good reasons for people to forgive others who've done them wrong. To a large degree, I agree with the notion that forgiveness is generally a healthy step to take when someone was wronged, whether or not the offender ever apologizes for their actions. Often, failure to forgive can lead to internal anguish for the person who isn't forgiving, and this can lead to more stress and painful emotions. In reality, it's often the case that a person who hurt you doesn't really care much whether you've forgiven them or not, so there's truth to the notion that withholding forgiveness has more of an impact on you than it does on the other person.

On the other hand, in line with the importance of each survivor's healing journey being an individual process, I believe the decision whether or not to forgive someone—whether your abuser or anyone else who hurt you along the way—should always be a decision you make for yourself. This decision also likely has a lot to do with how you define and understand forgiveness. If you view forgiveness as totally letting them off the hook for what they've done, that feels different than viewing forgiveness as a personal process of deciding to no longer allow another person's hurtful behaviors to continue to have control over your thoughts and emotions.

As such, once you've worked through other steps toward understanding and addressing hurtful experiences, consider what forgiveness means to you, and whether forgiveness is something you want to work toward in each specific relationship that's affected you. Think back to your understanding of the Trauma Backpack, and consider what would be the healthiest long-term way for you to come to a sense of closure or resolution with respect to the hurts you've faced. Your decisions in this area—as with all others—should be ones that make you feel most at peace with your experiences, as well as offer you the best chance for building a positive future.

Building and Growing Positive Social Support

Now that we've walked through steps for overcoming hurtful experiences in relationships, it's time to shift our focus to building more positive relationships that offer valuable support along your journey of triumphing over abuse. In addition to offering support, healthy relationships are important for many other reasons, including bringing meaning and joy to your life, providing companionship for enjoying new experiences, and allowing you to feel connected to a community. It's important to be intentional about building a positive, supportive network of people around you.

Let's face it, though … People who've been abused and mistreated can find it difficult to trust others, including in a romantic context, but also in other relationships, such as with friends, family members, and coworkers. Learning to trust again after your trust has been horrifically violated is no easy task. The aftermath of abuse can leave survivors feeling like they're always on edge in relationships, as well as highly sensitive about how others might be judging you and what they could say that could hurt you. Some people understandably make the choice to keep people at a distance to avoid getting hurt again, but this approach can lead to loneliness and isolation. In this section, we'll focus on decisions you can make to build a safe, supportive social network. As you read through the decisions below, think through what your next steps will be as you work on building a lasting, healthy social support system.

Decide to Accept that Relationships Always Come with a Risk of Being Hurt

The possibility of being hurt is inherent in any relationship. Hearing someone say, "I'll never hurt you," can sound comforting, but realistically, this is an ideal aspiration for relationships that's difficult, if not impossible, to achieve in reality. Any time you bring two or more people together in a relationship of any kind, there's a likelihood that differences, conflict, or pain could arise. In fact, the closer you become to another person, the more deeply they could hurt you. Although accepting that the risk of hurt is a natural part of relationships can seem like a sad, bleak view of relationships, this acceptance can be empowering and help you make wiser choices about relationships.

Accepting this risk of hurt in relationships is really an acceptance of your and others' humanity. Each of us is human, and this means we'll make mistakes from time to time (some of us more often than others!). Sometimes, we all act first out of our own self-interest, and this means our choices can be hurtful to others. Personally, I find it reassuring to know that we'll all make mistakes, and this helps me be patient and give grace *to* others—just as I know that I'll need patience and grace *from* others at times as well!

Conflict and differences of opinion are a normal part of any human relationships—but the good news is they can be managed and overcome in healthy relationships. By accepting the inevitability of conflict and challenges in relationships, you can take steps to prevent major hurts, as well as to protect yourself and learn to grow through hurtful experiences when they arise. Some specific ways you can do this are described in the other decisions described below (taking time to get to know people and setting healthy boundaries, for example). But, the most important thing you can bring to your relationships to address and overcome the risk of hurt is a healthier, stronger version of yourself. You are the constant factor in all your relationships, and by working to develop yourself personally, you're making an important investment in your ability to build safe, healthy relationships.

Remember: You are not the same person today who you used to be—and you're going to keep growing stronger and wiser for the rest of your life. You've faced hurt and trauma at the hands of at least one person who was supposed to love and support you. If you're afraid to face the risk of being hurt again, that is totally understandable! But, you can keep growing your confidence in your ability to face this risk by continuing to work on building your sense of self-worth, making wise choices about the people you get to know, and applying relationship skills to help navigate conflict and challenges in a healthy way. Along with deciding to accept the risk of possible hurts that can arise in relationships, decide to remind yourself that you're strong enough to face possible and actual hurts, work through them, and build stronger relationships with yourself and others in the process.

Decide to Free Yourself from Old "Rules" about Friendships and Relationships

Do you remember the old childhood song about new friends being silver and old friends being gold? It's certainly true that long-lasting, healthy, supportive friendships are extremely valuable. However, just because relationships have been around a long time, doesn't necessarily mean they still add value to your life. In fact, sometimes long-term friendships can become toxic and unhealthy. As you move into this next phase of your healing journey, it's important to think critically about the old "rules" you've been following about friendships and other types of relationships. This also includes examining the expectations you have about relationships, including romantic relationships.

Rules and expectations can be very helpful and healthy—such as if you have a personal rule to no longer tolerate abuse or disrespectful behavior in relationships. These kinds of healthy guidelines are important to establish for yourself. However, other rules and expectations that people can come to believe and follow might increase their chance of getting and staying involved in unhealthy, toxic relationships. We learn these rules about relationships from many sources, such as culture, society, media, advertising, and from the people who are influential in our lives.

Thinking critically about the relationship "rules" you've been following doesn't necessarily mean you'll abandon all of your previous values. Rather, it can mean you're more intentional about when and how you apply them, as well as more aware of ways they might be increasing your risk of unhealthy relationships. Think through some of the rules or expectations you've been following that may no longer be healthy, or that you may be following too rigidly. You may find it helpful to take out a piece of paper and write down a list of these rules, along with writing out questions to challenge the assumptions underlying those beliefs. As an example, consider the following list of possible

rules someone may be following, along with an alternate way of looking at
each expectation:

- I should always have one best friend in my life. *Perhaps I could enjoy several different close friendships and not be dependent on one specific person or relationship.*
- It's important to be popular and have a group of friends who I can go on girls' nights and trips on. *Some people have a large group of friends that all hang out together, but others enjoy one-on-one friendships with people who don't necessarily all hang out together. There's not one right way to have a group of friends.*
- I need to keep my dating life a secret from friends and family until I know a relationship is really serious. *Maybe, if I open up to close friends and family members while I'm in the dating process, they could help me make healthy decisions about how to approach dating relationships.*
- I need to have a set timeline for marriage. If I've been dating someone for a year, it's time to either get married or end the relationship if the other person isn't ready to commit. *Romantic relationships don't all follow the same timeline. Feeling like I have to be on a set timeline might make me feel pressured to move faster in a relationship than I feel comfortable with.*

Do any of these examples of rules and expectations seem familiar to you? Are there others you're holding onto that are impacting how you approach relationships in your life? It's not necessarily a bad thing to have expectations for your relationships—but it *is* important to be aware of how you've been living out these expectations, and how this influences the health of your relationships. Keep in mind there are a lot of ways to build healthy relationships and a positive social support system. Grant yourself permission to build the types of relationships that are the healthiest for you at this point in time—even if they may not look like what your previous rules and expectations allowed.

Decide to Let Your Relationships be Driven by Positive Motives, Not by Fear, Loneliness, or Desperation

In the journey to healing from abuse, there will be lonely days and nights. Sometimes, the loneliness can feel almost unbearable. There also will be moments where fears surround you—including fears of being alone and not having close relationships with others. You may have moments when you'll wonder how you'll make it through the next ten minutes, let alone the next ten days or weeks. I wish I could tell you there was some easy way to make it through these dark, lonely times. The truth is, it's not easy to make it through them, although in time it can start to feel easier as you begin seeing the strength you're gaining in the process, and that you *can* make it through these times, even if it challenges you to your core.

In moments of fear, loneliness, or desperation, you may be tempted to make unhealthy choices, such as engaging in risky coping mechanisms. The temptation also may arise to find someone, *anyone*, to spend time with so you that won't feel so alone. As much as it's important to reach out for support when you're feeling down, it's also critical to be cautious against reaching out for connection with someone who may provide temporary relief, but ultimately will mean bad news for you in the long-term. Of course, this could be true when it comes to a toxic romantic relationship, but desperation and loneliness also can lead you to lean into unhealthy relationships with friends, family members, coworkers, and others who might hurt you or have a negative influence on you.

Survivors often learn difficult, but important life lessons about loneliness through their abusive relationships. For example: It's better to be by yourself than to be with another person who mistreats you. Another example: Just because you have a partner, doesn't mean you don't feel alone. In fact, one of the loneliest places you can be is in a relationship with a person who treats you badly. Even still, the pain of loneliness can drive people to make pretty unhealthy decisions about relationships. That's why it's so important to make relationship decisions based on positive motives, rather than an attempt to find temporary relief from loneliness and fear.

There are some important questions you can ask yourself when you find yourself in a state of loneliness and considering making a choice about a relationship you're not sure about—such as texting someone who you know isn't good for you, going on a date with someone who shows red flags of being abusive, or starting to gossip or stir up trouble with a coworker:

- Do I genuinely want to make a positive connection with this person, or am I just reaching out because I'm lonely?
- What could be the negative consequences of interacting with this person?
- How will I feel about making this decision tomorrow, or a week from now?
- Is there something else I could do now, or a person that I could reach out to, that would lead to healthier consequences?

Be extra cautious about how you engage in relationships with others when you're feeling down. Let your relationship choices be driven by positive motives, such as a desire to build a positive connection with someone, excitement about getting to know that person better, and a sense of meaning and fulfilment that comes from your relationship. Use your coping tools to help you get through the difficult moments so you can be in a healthy place when you're faced with decisions about how and with whom you spend your precious time and energy in relationships.

Decide to Take Time to Get to Know People and Build Relationships Slowly

Whether you're starting to build new relationships with people you just met or rebuilding trust in a relationship that has been challenging, prepare to take the process of building and rebuilding relationships slowly. It takes time to really get to know people. Stephen Covey, the author of *The 7 Habits of Highly Successful People*, said, "When it comes to people, fast is slow and slow is fast."[3] There simply is no shortcut to building strong, lasting relationships with others. In fact, University of Kansas researcher Jeffrey Hall did a study[4] that showed that it takes over 200 hours together for people to become close friends!

Knowing that close relationships can take so much time to develop can feel frustrating, especially if you're excited to build a new social network for this next phase of life. However, try to value the time spent building your relationships with others, even if it feels awkward at times as you're learning about and becoming more comfortable with each other. The slow approach to getting to know people serves an important protective mechanism, as it offers time and space to build trust and get to know the other person's true character, while you allow them to get to know you better during that same timeframe. People who are worth building lasting relationships with will stand the test of time—and if relationships don't progress because of taking things slowly, then it may not have been the kind of relationship you want to be in anyways.

Decide to Be Intentional about Who You Give Access to Your Innermost Circles

Think about your social support system as a group of concentric circles. Your closest circles represent the people you allow to get closest to you, and your farthest circles represent people with whom you have more distant relationships—either because you don't interact with them very much, or because you intentionally want to keep them at a farther distance. Each person can choose the number of social circles that feels right to them, but it might be helpful to think about your closest circle, your medium circle, and your distant circle. Know that it's your choice the extent to which you grant people access to your innermost thoughts and feelings, as well as with whom you choose to invest the greatest amounts of time and energy.

It's wise to be fiercely protective over who you allow in your innermost circle. It's also normal if your innermost circle is relatively small, such as a few close friends and family members. It's also fine if you have a larger inner circle. The key is to choose to allow people into your inner circle based on the *quality* of their character, rather than on some notion about the *quantity* of people you want to keep close. Intentionally seek out close relationships with people who have good character—which, as discussed above, is typically revealed gradually over an extended period of time. Reflect on the characteristics that you'd like to see in people who are close to you, such as honesty, dependability, compassion, and kindness. If someone reveals themself to lack the essential character qualities that are important to you, know it's okay to keep greater distance from them—both emotionally and physically.

Decide to Practice Healthy Boundaries in Relationships of All Kinds

As we discussed earlier in this chapter, healthy boundaries are both about keeping bad things out and allowing good things in. Building and maintaining healthy boundaries in relationships isn't a one-time deal. In fact, boundary issues can be an especially frustrating part of relationships because they can take a lot of time and effort to establish.

Take time to grow in your understanding of healthy vs. unhealthy boundaries. One helpful resource is the book, *Boundaries,*[5] by Drs. Henry Cloud and John Townsend, although this book is written from a Christian perspective, so it may not be useful for people from other spiritual backgrounds. Through the Healthy Relationships Initiative that I direct, we've also put out a popular blog post that offers some useful insights: https://www.guilfordhri.org/healthy-vs-unhealthy-boundaries/.

Some theoretical approaches to family counseling—Family Systems Theory, and Structural Family Therapy in particular—also offer helpful insights into what healthy boundaries look like. Generally speaking, healthy boundaries have the right balances between (1) individuality and closeness and

(2) flexibility and stability, and the balance is aligned with the nature of the relationship. For example, the boundary between a newborn baby and its parents is healthiest when it's very close, as a baby is almost entirely dependent on its parents to meet its needs. In contrast, the boundary between partners in a romantic relationship is likely healthiest when it gives space for each person's individuality, but also provides enough emotional and physical closeness to keep their relationship strong. Likewise, healthy boundaries in most types of relationships have enough flexibility to adapt to changing needs and circumstances, but also enough stability to provide consistency and dependability between the people in the relationship. In the process of building a strong, healthy support network, practice using effective relationship skills, like communication and conflict management, to build and sustain healthy boundaries.

Decide to Build a Diverse Social Network that Offers Different Kinds of Support and Experiences

Keeping in mind what we discussed above about being intentional about who to allow into your innermost social circle, there's also value in building as large and diverse of a social network as you are comfortable with. It's okay to have supportive people even on the outskirts of your social network, as different people offer different types of support to your life. Try to have as many positive, supportive people in your corner as you're going through your healing journey, and remember you also can find meaning in relationships by offering help and encouragement to people in your network as well, which we'll talk more in Chapter 10.

The list below offers ideas about diverse types of people and relationships to consider including in your social network:

- *Professional Helpers.* This may include counselors or therapists for yourself and your children, a victim advocate, medical professionals, attorneys, staff of crisis lines, and teachers or other school personnel who work with your children.
- *Friends and Family Members.* Cultivate close relationships with friends and family members who have proven to be reliable at offering support. If they don't know a lot about the process of recovering from abuse, consider educating them on the process so they can understand what you're going through. To build new friendships, consider trying out clubs, activity groups, and classes in your community.

- *Coworkers and/or Classmates.* You spend a lot of time at work (or at school if you're pursuing a degree or certificate), so consider getting to know kind people you interact with in those settings. These relationships may not always be the closest ones in your life, but they can offer support in your work and educational endeavors, and also help you enjoy those experiences more in the process.
- *Support Groups.* Many domestic violence support groups are geared more toward people who more recently left an abusive relationship. However, it's possible you can find a group specific to longer-term survivors in your community, as well as other general support groups, such as those focusing on empowering women or addressing parenting concerns. Another powerful source of support in today's world is online support groups and social media pages geared toward survivors. Just be sure to be cautious about privacy issues when sharing personal information online.
- *Community Connections.* You can find supportive people and relationships in virtually any aspect of your community, such as a faith community, your neighborhood, the gym, and even your favorite coffee shop. Be open to meeting and connecting with people in all areas of your life. Remember that not every relationship has to turn into a very close friendship to add to your life.

Decide to Make the Best Decisions for Yourself about Pursuing Future Romantic Relationships

The decision about whether and when to consider a new romantic relationship after experiencing an abusive relationship can be a tricky one. Some people decide never to try again for another romantic relationship after facing hurt in their past abusive relationship. However, others remain hopeful about finding and building a loving, supportive partnership. This is another area in which each person needs to carefully decide the best approach to future romantic relationships for themselves. It's okay to decide to not pursue another romantic relationship, either temporarily or ever again. However, if you're considering a decision to never again be open to a future romantic relationship, think about whether that decision is one that is based on fears that you could overcome if the right person came along and if you had a desire for romantic love in your life.

It's also wise to be careful about running too quickly into another relationship in the aftermath of an abusive relationship—or really in the aftermath of any significant relationship. It takes time to heal from the end of a meaningful romantic relationship, and rushing into another relationship might mean you'll bring open wounds into the next relationship that might negatively impact that relationship. Through See the Triumph, we've built a whole Collection on the topic of building safe, healthy relationships following abuse, which you can check out here: http://www.seethetriumph.org/collection-safe-and-healthy-relationships-following-abuse.html.

If you decide to stay open to building a new romantic relationship, two helpful approaches including taking things slowly and building a "committee" of close friends or family members to help you make decisions. We've already discussed the benefits of taking relationships slowly above, and the benefits of the slow approach are especially evident in romantic relationships. In fact, many abusers take the approach of quickly pursuing a prospective victim and building a fast relationship as a way to entrap someone in a relationship. Of course, not all relationships that move quickly are abusive, but when someone tries winning you over and making the relationship move forward quickly, that should be considered a red flag of possible abuse. By moving slowly as you explore a possible romantic relationship with a new prospective partner, you're setting the tone for the relationship to grow steadily over time, while also giving yourself time to look for other red flags and see if this is the type of person that you'd feel safe and comfortable getting close with.

I first heard the concept of "building a committee" when I was presenting a training on domestic violence many years ago. I wish I had gotten the name of the person who said this idea, but all I remember is that it came up during a panel of survivors that happened during lunchtime between the morning and afternoon sessions of the training. One of the panelists said something to the extent of, "If you're going to consider dating after you've been in an abusive relationship, then what you need to do is put together a committee to help you along the way." Probably because of my years working in a university setting, where there are tons of committees on virtually every topic, I loved the idea of establishing a committee to help survivors along the process of dating and building a new romantic relationship.

If you've been involved with an abusive partner, it's natural to question your ability to pick a quality partner. Of course, most abusers are pretty deceptive and present as good partners at first, and they typically do have some good qualities and aren't abusive 100% of the time. Even if you've accepted that the abuse wasn't your fault and that it made sense you were attracted to your abuser at the start of your relationship, it would be understandable to have doubts about whether you can trust yourself in picking a partner. Even if you feel confident in your picking skills, it's not a bad idea to enlist the support of people who support and care for you. It's normal early in a romantic relationship to be caught up in the emotions and excitement and overlook possible problems.

Building a committee doesn't have to be as formal of a process as it sounds. It may be as simple as asking one or two close friends or family members if they'd be willing to talk with you about your experiences with dating and help you think through decisions, as well as to be honest with you about their impressions of someone you're dating if they meet them. But also, feel free to have fun and be creative with this idea. You might even have official committee "meetings" and let your prospective partner know they'll have to have an "interview" with your committee (even if the interview is just a friendly conversation over a meal). A prospective partner who is really interested in getting to know you may feel a bit nervous if they know you've got a committee, but if they really like you, they should be up for meeting your friends and family and taking the steps needed to help you feel comfortable moving forward in the relationship.

Pursuing another possible romantic relationship after you've been hurt in a previous one is a brave thing to do. Although it can be scary, keeping an open mind to a future relationship is a way to take ownership of your future, whether it includes another romantic relationship or not. As you consider taking steps toward another intimate relationship, be sure to take things slowly, seek guidance from supportive people in your life, and make decisions in the relationship that feel safe and comfortable to you.

Summary

Learning to make all of these decisions toward building a healthy support network can take time, and there definitely will be frustrating (and sometimes downright painful) moments along the way. Taking steps toward building a diverse, healthy support system can be especially daunting in the aftermath of difficult past relationship experiences. One of the most exciting things about the process of building a supportive social network is that it truly is a lifelong process. Your relationships will evolve and change as you go through different phases of life and your recovery journey. Sometimes, relationships or friendships that were close at one point will end, and this can be a sad experience. But new, positive relationships may be just around the corner. By staying open to new relationships and continuing to make choices and take actions that foster healthy relationships, you have the potential to experience many different types of meaningful relationships throughout the rest of your life.

References

1. Crowe, A., & Murray, C. E. (2015). Stigma from professional helpers toward survivors of intimate partner violence. *Partner Abuse, 6(2)*, p. 157–179.

   Murray, C. E., Crowe, A., & Brinkley, J. (2015). The stigma surrounding intimate partner violence: A cluster analysis study. *Partner Abuse, 6(3)*, 320–336.

   Murray, C. E., Crowe, A., & Overstreet, N. (2015). Sources and components of stigma experienced by survivors of intimate partner violence. *Journal of Interpersonal Violence, 33*, 515–536. DOI:10.1177/0886260515609565

2. Murray, C. E., Crowe, A., & Overstreet, N. (2015). Sources and components of stigma experienced by survivors of intimate partner violence. *Journal of Interpersonal Violence, 33*, 515–536. DOI:10.1177/0886260515609565

3. Franklin Covey Content Team (2019). Slow down. Retrieved June 26, 2020, from https://resources.franklincovey.com/leadership-tips/slow-down.

4. Hall, J. (2018). How many hours does it take to make a friend? *Journal of Social and Personal Relationships*. DOI:10.1177/0265407518761225. https://www.researchgate.net/publication/323783184_How_many_hours_does_it_take_to_make_a_friend

5. Cloud, H., & Townsend, J. (2017). *Boundaries*. Grand Rapids, MI: Zondervan.

4
EDUCATING YOURSELF ABOUT ABUSE

> "I believe you have to realize that although you made mistakes in the relationship, the abuser was setting you up to take all the blame from day one. There was an imbalance of power and you reacted to it. People were hurt because of your inability to leave. Forgiving yourself for these things is the first step to recovery. Looking ahead and not staying stuck behind is the next step."
>
> ~ Domestic Violence Survivor

It's normal for survivors to feel very alone about their experiences, especially if they don't know many other people who've been in an abusive relationship. One way to feel less alone is to learn more about how common abuse is, as well as common dynamics of abuse. Knowledge is power, and this is especially true when it comes to learning about abuse. Educating yourself about abuse is empowering because it can help you understand your past experiences better, as well as gain confidence as you move forward into future relationships so you can understand signs of a potential abuser to look out for.

As you continue learning more about abuse throughout this chapter and in other ways beyond the information in this book, don't condemn yourself or feel ashamed for things you didn't know before. Even if you had all the knowledge in the world about abuse, there's still a possibility of getting involved with an abusive partner. Remember that abusers can be very manipulative and deceptive, and the "real world" dynamics of abuse often don't fit neatly into textbook descriptions of abusive relationships. Abusive relationships all have some common characteristics, but every experience of abuse has unique aspects as well. Therefore, universal definitions of abuse often miss some of the more individualized experiences that survivors face.

In this chapter, we'll start by covering basic dynamics of abusive relationships, and then we'll turn our attention to aspects of abusive relationships that aren't as widely understood. But first, check out the following quotes from survivors who participated in our See the Triumph research[1] that further underscore the importance of educating yourself about abuse during the recovery process:

> "Find out how an abuser and victim are created. Find out what healthy families and relationships truly are. Be brave enough to look at yourself and your family honestly and deal with the ugliness of dysfunction."

> "One thing I would love to see done on college campuses is more awareness about domestic violence, because so much of it occurs during the college years, whether they live on campus or not. So much of it occurs then."

> "I think the biggest driving force for me is that I had done enough studying and had enough exposure to dysfunctional situations, that I knew the only way to give them a chance was to leave and to break the cycle. So, and again, in my frame or my circle of people there was no understanding of that."

As these quotes illustrate, education can be crucial for taking steps forward in the recovery process, as well as for learning to break intergenerational patterns of abuse in families.

Understanding Abusive Relationships: The Basics

Most likely, if you've had any training on domestic violence or sought help from a domestic violence agency, you've seen the Power and Control Wheel, which was developed by the Domestic Abuse Intervention Programs in Duluth, Minnesota. If you haven't yet seen the Power and Control Wheel, you can find it at https://www.theduluthmodel.org/wheels/, where you also can download translated versions of the wheel in a number of languages. The Power and Control Wheel is an important educational tool because it illustrates one of the most important defining characteristics of abusive relationships: *Abusive relationships are characterized by the abusive partner's attempts to gain power and control over the other person.*

Another common concept discussed in educational resources about abusive relationships is called the Cycle of Violence, which describes three phases that happen in abusive relationships: the tension-building phase, the explosion or violent incident phase, and the honeymoon phase. I remember first learning about the Cycle of Violence in a graduate school class on family violence, and then I couldn't believe how commonly I saw that very cycle play out among counseling clients with whom I worked who had current or past experiences of abuse. This Cycle of Violence illustrates how serious incidents of violence or abuse often occur after a period of increasing tension within the relationship, and then after the abuse occurs, an abuser may become apologetic, make promises to change or never be hurtful again, and do romantic gestures like buying gifts or flowers. Over time, the honeymoon phase often fades after the abusive partner has established control, and the cycle typically escalates over time. Early in the relationship, the explosion or violent incident may be simply a hurtful word, and over time it can grow to lethal physical violence.

Even understanding these two foundational aspects of abusive relationships—power and control dynamics of abuse and the cycle of violence—can go a long way toward helping to understand your experiences of abuse. When you begin to understand the extent to which your abuser went to gain power and control over you, you might start to think differently about your own behaviors and thoughts within that relationship and how much they were controlled or manipulated by your partner. Likewise, seeing how a pattern of abuse, apologies, and romantic gestures played out in your relationship can help you understand how you became more and more trapped within that relationship. Because you loved and cared for your partner, you wanted to believe their apologies and that their love for you would overcome the hurts they caused. For these two concepts and any others you learn, I encourage you to reflect on how learning new information can help you gain new insights into your experiences.

There are other foundational characteristics that are important to review before we move on to some less widely-understood aspects of abusive relationships. First, there are many different types of abuse, including physical, sexual, emotional, verbal, psychological, stalking, technology-facilitated, and financial. Examples of the types of behaviors that might fall into each of these categories are provided below:

- *Physical Abuse.* Hitting, kicking, biting, strangulation, using weapons, punching, choking, and using physical threats or intimidation
- *Sexual Abuse.* Forcing or coercing you to engage in any form of sexual activity, forced participation or viewing of pornography, and videotaping sexual acts without consent
- *Emotional Abuse.* Playing on your emotions, treating you like your feelings and emotions don't matter, and using fear or shame as a means of control
- *Verbal Abuse.* Using words to hurt, name-calling, aggressive language, verbal threats, and discrediting your thoughts or opinions
- *Psychological Abuse.* Playing mind games, gaslighting (i.e., attempting to falsely convince you that something you think happened didn't actually happen), manipulation, and trying to make you think you are crazy
- *Stalking.* Tracking or following you without your consent—either in person or via technology—such as using GPS to monitor your whereabouts
- *Technology-facilitated Abuse.* Harassing you through email or text messages, setting up fake social media profiles in your name, monitoring your online activity without permission, and installing ghost apps onto your phone or tablet
- *Financial Abuse.* Committing identity fraud, restricting access to financial resources or information, stealing money, and hindering your ability to work or pursue educational opportunities

A relationship can be abusive if it contains one or more of these types of abuse. Some people mistakenly believe a relationship has to include physical violence to be considered abusive, but the truth is any and all forms of abuse can be very traumatic for survivors. I don't think it's possible to say that any one type of abuse is universally more harmful for survivors. Physical violence can be terrifying, especially if it puts your life at risk. However, we've also heard from many survivors in our research that emotional and psychological abuse can be just as, if not more, difficult to heal from due to the internal bruises they can leave.

Most, if not all, abusive relationships include at least some degree of emotional abuse. It's difficult to imagine an abuser would use any of the other abuse tactics without also inflicting emotional hurt and control. This is an important piece of information to keep in mind as you move throughout your recovery process: Most likely, in addition to other impacts of the abuse you've faced, there will be emotional consequences to work through related to emotional abuse you faced.

Emotional abuse often is a precursor to other forms of abuse, and this is part of how an abuser starts to establish control over their partner. Although emotional abuse can escalate to other forms of abuse, this doesn't happen in all relationships, and a relationship can be abusive even if physical or sexual violence never occur. Even without any other forms of abuse, emotionally abusive relationships can be very complex and traumatic. However, abusive relationships and the subsequent recovery process can become even more complex when more and more layers of abuse become compounded on top of one another. Every type of abuse you faced will likely translate into added layers of healing to work through.

If you faced other types of abuse that weren't included in the list above, you're not alone! Having heard the stories of many, many survivors through my work, I can tell you that abusers can truly come up with any number of tragically creative ways to hurt their partners. There are countless types of abuse tactics abusers might use to hurt and control their partners, so don't let the categories and definitions get too rigid in your mind.

Abuse can look different in every situation. Some abusers use more traditional weapons, like their fists or a knife. Others turn everyday household objects like books or pillows into weapons. Some abusers use more common hurtful words, such as "You're stupid," or "You're ugly." For others, verbal abuse can look like making fun of the TV shows you watch or criticizing a nice meal you made. One of the reasons abuse can go on for a long time is because it often doesn't look like a black eye or blatantly mean words. It's often only in hindsight that survivors realize the extent to which their partners' words and actions reflected an abusive relationship. Let this knowledge empower you to know that, if you didn't immediately recognize that your relationship was abusive, you are not alone.

Indeed, as a survivor of abuse, you're certainly not alone, and before moving on from this section, one final basic piece of information that's important to understand is just how common intimate partner violence and abuse are. According to the CDC's National Intimate Partner and Sexual Violence Survey,[2] a quarter of women and one-tenth of men in the United States have experienced negative impacts from physical, sexual and/or stalking abuse by an intimate partner at some point in their lives. When you also include psychological aggression, over one-third of both women and men have experienced abusive behaviors in intimate relationships in their lifetimes. As of March 2020, the population of the U.S. was over 329 million people. Based on the CDC's survey projections, this means that over 109 million adults in the country have faced any form of intimate partner abuse, and over 82 million women and over 32 million men have faced physical violence, sexual violence, or stalking. Truly, if you faced abuse by an intimate partner, know that you are not alone—even if sometimes it feels lonely along your journey to recovery.

Understanding Abusive Relationships: A Deeper Dive

Now that we've covered some basic facts about abusive relationships, it's time to turn our attention to aspects of abuse that aren't as widely understood, but that can be very important to understand as survivors move forward in their process of triumphing over abuse. Unfortunately, there are common stereotypes about abuse that just aren't true, and these stereotypes can hinder survivors' recovery.

In addition to challenging stereotypes, it's also important for survivors to understand some of the more subtle aspects of abusive relationships that go beyond understanding the big ideas, like underlying power and control dynamics and the cycle of violence. This has been one of the most powerful aspects of our research related to the See the Triumph campaign. As we've listened to so many survivors' stories, we've heard about aspects of abuse and the recovery process that don't typically show up in a textbook or training programs about domestic violence.

Survivors definitely can move forward in their healing journey without understanding these more subtle experiences. However, when survivors realize they're not alone in their experiences, the healing process can be enhanced. It's the power of the moment of realizing, "I'm not the only one who went through this." To explore some of these more subtle aspects of abusive relationships, this section will dive deeper into common lived experiences that survivors might* face, and we'll use the "I'm not the only one who..." statement as our framework for exploring these experiences. (*Note: Because every survivor's experience with abuse is unique, not all of the following dynamics will apply to every reader. Consider the experiences that you can relate to, and read the others with an eye toward gaining understanding of what other survivors may face that is different from your own experiences.)

"I'm Not the Only One ... from Cultural/Educational/ Ethnic/Socioeconomic Background who Faced Abuse"

Stereotypes about abuse can lead people to believe that only certain types of people face abuse. These stereotypes can become internalized for survivors, which might lead them to feel ashamed about abuse happening to "people like me." When people have an image in their mind of what types of people experience abuse, and those images don't match up with how they view themselves, this can make it harder to recognize abuse when it's happening, as well as present challenges for the healing process after the abusive relationship ends.

For example, I remember one of the very first survivors that I interviewed for our See the Triumph-related research studies (long before the See the Triumph campaign even existed). This survivor described horrific physical, sexual, and emotional abuse that was both life-threatening and demoralizing. However, when I asked her about what help she sought out for support, she said she didn't think that resources like the local domestic violence agency were set up for people like her. I remember feeling quite shocked when she told me she didn't want to trouble those resources because she thought there were other people who needed the help more than her—and this was right after she described the terrible extent to which she'd been abused. The image this survivor—along with many, many other survivors—held in her mind about who could and could not be considered a victim of domestic violence kept her from reaching out for help and taking steps toward safety for a long time.

Stereotypes about what types of people experience abuse also add challenges in the recovery process. Survivors may face feelings of shame and embarrassment, a sense of secrecy or fear that others can't find out what happened, and difficulty acknowledging the extent of abuse they faced. In addition, these stereotypes can add challenges to accessing support from survivors' support networks, especially if friends, family members, or professionals in those networks also hold stereotypical viewpoints about abuse. This could lead people who might be able to offer valuable support to minimize or dismiss the extent of the abuse, as well as keep them from understanding the available resources for support in the community.

The truth about domestic violence is that anyone, from any background, can become victimized by an abusive partner. I've met or heard the stories of many survivors, and I've seen that survivors come from virtually every socioeconomic, educational, racial, ethnic, professional, geographic, religious, and any other background demographic. As one of the survivors in our research said, "Do not think that because you are beautiful, educated, creative, intelligent, or rich that you are immune to abuse."

These stereotypes about abuse can be difficult to work through, but doing so can be an important part of the healing process. In my own healing journey, one of the most powerful mental shifts I made was deciding I wasn't going to carry around the shame of the abuse that rightly belonged to my abuser. That included not feeling ashamed that someone from my educational, religious, and family background could have been abused. Admittedly, it was much easier to make this decision than it was to actually live it out, and there are still days when I have to remind myself to release the shame again. However, it's critical for survivors to continue to remind ourselves of the truth that having been abused isn't a result of personal defects or faults, but that our abuse was fully the responsibility of the abuser.

Along with understanding that abuse can happen to anyone, it's also important to remember the corresponding truth that *abusers* can come from virtually any background, too. Just as wealth, a high education, and good looks can't guarantee that someone won't become a victim, these same characteristics—wealth, education, and attractiveness—can't guarantee a person will not be an abuser. Abusive people also come from all walks of life, too. The sad truth is that you can't tell just by looking at someone if they are or could become abusive. This can be a scary realization, but it's also one that underscores the importance of taking time to get to know people, as we discussed in the last chapter. It also leads us to the next truth about abusive relationships that we'll cover.

"I'm Not the Only One Who ... Thought My Relationship Started Out Like It Would Become a Wonderful Relationship"

People often wonder why someone gets involved with an abusive partner. But, the truth is, healthy and abusive relationships often look very similar at the start of the relationship. Most people probably wouldn't accept a second date if their date hit them or called them names on the first date. Just like in healthy relationships, people who eventually become abusive typically present the best version of themselves to prospective partners early in the relationship. In fact, early in a relationship that becomes abusive, an abusive partner may even turn on the charm even more as part of the overall pattern of manipulation that eventually turns into controlling behaviors.

In many cases, people end up getting deeply involved with their partners before any signs of abuse begin. I've even spoken with people who didn't see any signs of abuse until after they were married to their partners. But even if abusive behaviors appear long before the couple has made a deep commitment like marriage, there's another relationship dimension that can lead people to overlook early signs of abuse: feelings and affection. In fact, some of the earliest signs of an abusive partner can even come across as signs of affection. For example, giving a lot of attention to you or wanting to spend a lot of time together could be signs of genuine love and care—but they also could be signs of someone who is controlling and possessive.

Generally speaking, people get involved with abusive relationships in much the same way they become involved in healthy relationships. They start spending time together, getting to know each other, and developing feelings for each other. Even in healthy relationships, everybody is human and imperfect, so partners face conflict and learn to accept each other's differences. The feelings and affection that grows between partners helps them stay together through difficult times, and this is no less true for people in abusive relationships. The key difference between healthy and abusive relationships is the actions and choices of abusive partners. In healthy relationships, both partners treat each other with respect and kindness. But in abusive relationships, one partner doesn't do this, and instead uses words and behaviors designed to gain power and control, as we discussed earlier.

Understanding that abusive and healthy relationships often start out in much the same ways can be eye-opening for survivors. It's freeing to understand that it wasn't a lack of intelligence that led you to get involved with your abusive partner, but rather you were trying to build a healthy, loving relationship, but with a person who couldn't offer the same to you.

"I'm Not the Only One Who ... Had a Partner that Wasn't a Terrible Person All the Time"

We just talked about how abusive relationships often start out looking similar to healthy relationships, and this helps explain how people end up getting involved with abusive partners in the first place. This then leads us to another question that people who don't fully understand the dynamics of abuse often ask, which is why people stay with an abusive partner once abuse begins. There are many reasons someone may stay in an abusive relationship, including that it may be unsafe to leave, the survivor may not have access to financial resources to leave, and staying together might feel like the best choice because the couple has children together.

In addition to those reasons, one of the lesser-known truths about abusive relationships that also can contribute to people staying with abusive partners is that abusive relationships typically aren't abusive 100% of the time. In fact, there are often times in a relationship with an abusive partner that feel neutral, or even positive when things are going well. This was a big part of my personal experience in my relationship with my abuser, and it contributed to a lot of my confusion about the relationship. There were times when things would get really bad, and I would feel awful about the relationship (and often about myself, too). But then, his behaviors would change into being either not-so-bad or even positive, and sometimes these calmer periods would last for weeks or even months on end. During those times, I would think to myself, "Well, maybe this relationship isn't all that bad after all? Maybe he was just in a bad mood?" I would hold out hope during those moments that things were turning around, but just like we covered earlier in the discussion on the cycle of violence, eventually the abusive behaviors would show up again, and the cycle would start over again.

Of course, there are some abusers who are all-around evil people and don't really have any positive qualities. Some people are just nasty all the time, at least after their true character comes out if they put on a positive front while trying to lure their partner into the relationship. But, many abusive people do have positive personal characteristics. They may be smart, interesting, helpful around the house, or successful in their careers. They even may be leaders in their communities and highly regarded by others.

To be clear, there's no amount of good behavior or positive personal qualities that excuses away abusive behaviors. However, for victims currently in an abusive relationship who are trying for whatever reason (such as love, fear, or practical considerations) to make that relationship work, those positive aspects offer the glimmer of hope needed to make it through the day. They also can add a heavy dose of confusion about whether leaving or staying in the relationship is the right choice. For survivors in the aftermath of an abusive relationship, the recovery process often involves working through this confusion, as well as grieving the loss of the positive aspects of the relationship, which leads us to the next deeper truth we'll uncover about abusive relationships.

"I'm Not the Only One Who … Felt Sad when My Abusive Relationship Ended"

It would be logical to assume that someone who has managed to become free from an abusive partner would feel only happiness and joy about that relationship ending. In truth, however, the end of any relationship—even an abusive one—can lead to feelings of sadness and a lengthy grieving process. These grief-related feelings can add extra confusion, and they even may make a survivor question if they should return to the abuser, especially if that person is trying to win the relationship back.

It's natural to feel sadness about an abusive relationship ending. As we discussed above, abusive partners and relationships usually aren't all bad, all the time. This means it's understandable to feel sadness over positive memories of the relationship and over the dreams you had for the future of the relationship. There even may be times when you'll feel like you miss your abuser, as well as feelings of loneliness about being on your own.

Understanding that these feelings (along with positive feelings that also may come along with the relationship's end) are natural can help survivors move forward in the grieving and healing process. Just because you feel this sadness doesn't mean you liked or miss being abused. These feelings also don't mean it would be wise to return to a relationship with the person who abused you. However, these feelings do mean you're working through a significant change and loss in your life. Even losses of things that weren't healthy can require a grieving process in order to move forward to a more positive future.

"I'm Not the Only One Who ... Took a Long, Long Time to Truly Come to the End of My Abusive Relationship"

Grieving the end of an abusive relationship can be a lengthy process, and another important truth is that the end of abusive relationships often involves a protracted process that may include multiple attempts to reconcile with the abusive partner. People often talk about the end of an abusive relationship like it's a discrete, one-time event. This is the case for some people, but many survivors actually experience a long, painful end that involves periods of going in and out of the relationship before finally breaking free, once and for all.

I've heard the statistic many times that it takes a victim anywhere from 7 to 13 attempts to leave an abusive relationship before finally leaving for good. I've searched for the original source of that statistic, and I've not been able to find it, but I believe it's a good approximation of the number of times it takes to try and leave an abusive partner, and I've seen that pattern play out among survivors in my research, clinical work, and personal network. Regardless of whether it takes 1 or 100 attempts to leave an abusive partner, the end of a relationship with an abuser is rarely a quick, easy process.

A lot of people ask the question, "Why do people stay in abusive relationships?" However, an even more important question to ask is, "Why do people leave?" Several years ago, my colleagues and I became interested in this question, and we did a research study[3] to identify the turning points that led to survivors making the decision to end their relationships with their abusers, although sometimes it took time between the turning point decisions and the actual end of the relationship. This study involved 123 survivors of abuse, and we found six themes in their descriptions of the turning points leading to the end of their relationships, which included (1) being threatened with severe, possibly life-threatening violence, (2) having a shift in how they viewed their relationship, such as realizing the cruelty of their partner, (3) learning about patterns involved in abusive relationships, (4) having some sort of external intervention, such as involvement of police or a friend or family member expressing concern about the relationship, (5) realizing how their children were being hurt by the abuse, and (6) some other reason the relationship ended, such as their abuser breaking up with them, dying, or going to jail. Some survivors said they couldn't pinpoint a single turning point, and sometimes there were multiple layers of reasons that ultimately led to an abusive relationship's end.

You're not alone if the end of your abusive relationship was a long, drawn-out process. It doesn't mean you weren't strong enough to make a clean break. Rather, you were facing a delicate balance of having a lot of reasons to leave, but also a lot of reasons to stay. Once your relationship is behind you, be proud you made it out, however it happened.

"I'm Not the Only One Who … Has an Abuser Who Continues to Try and Hurt Me, Even Long After the Relationship Ended"

As long and harrowing the process of ending an abusive relationship can be, another important truth about abusive relationships is that often, just because the relationship has ended, it doesn't necessarily mean that the abuse has ended, too. We'll cover the topic of dealing with continued abuse in detail in Chapter 8. For now, it's important to acknowledge that the notion of an abusive relationship being over isn't always as clean and simple as it sounds. After a relationship with an abuser ends, the abuse can continue in an ongoing or sporadic way for a short or long time period. Also, for a brief or extended time, the abuse may even get worse after the relationship ends. This can be especially true in the immediate period after a survivor has left, when the risk of severe violence is often the highest.

This truth has important implications for your recovery process. It means you may have to deal with your past experiences, while the past continues to rear its ugly head in the present moment. It's important to be intentional about your healing process for the past abuse you faced, and also about protecting yourself against future abuse and healing from new abusive encounters that come up in the future. Ongoing abuse also means you may need to continue to address safety concerns, such as by continuous safety planning to address new safety risks as they arise. The potential for continued abuse is heightened when there are reasons you need to remain in contact with your abuser, such as ongoing legal processes or when children are involved. Custody exchanges and parenting issues can be especially high-risk situations for future abuse.

It can feel extremely frustrating—and perhaps even depressing—if you're facing ongoing abuse, even after the relationship ends. We'll address strategies for addressing ongoing abuse in Chapter 8, but for now, knowing you're not alone in this experience can be empowering. In particular, whether abuse occurs while you are in the relationship or after the relationship ended, it's always fully the responsibility of the abuser. Also, as you move forward in your recovery process, taking proactive steps to set boundaries with your abuser can be empowering. You'll learn new ways to interact with your abuser that help you continue to grow in your confidence and see that you can build a safe, happy life, regardless of how others treat you.

"I'm Not the Only One Who ... Doesn't Recognize the Person I Became when I Was in My Abusive Relationship"

A final important truth about abusive relationships reflects the toll they can take on victims and survivors: someone in an abusive relationship can become disconnected from their true self, but the recovery process can lead to an opportunity to rebuild your life in a way that is meaningful to you. It's common for people to feel like they became a shell of their former selves over the course of an abusive relationship. Abusers can wear their victims down and chip away at their self-esteem, interests, hobbies, friendships, and mental state. Dealing with an abusive partner is exhausting and energy-depleting. Most survivors are quite familiar with the emotional toll it takes to be under the constant stress and anxiety of not knowing what will set off their abusers next.

It's important for survivors to understand how disconnected they may have become from their true personality, thoughts, and feelings during their abusive relationship to help in the process of reevaluating their experiences during the recovery process. You may be looking back now that you're out of the relationship and having a hard time understanding some of the things you said or did, as well as decisions you made while you were in the relationship. It's normal to have these questions, but know that your mind probably wasn't as clear then as it is now, when you're safe and out of the relationship.

Don't feel ashamed if you had a foggy mind while facing the trauma of abuse, and don't despair if you felt like you didn't even know who you were when the relationship ended. These are normal experiences that reflect the dangerous, emotionally taxing, and socially isolating dynamics of abusive relationships. Becoming disconnected from your sense of self is difficult, but it also presents an opportunity for you to rebuild a new version of yourself in the recovery process that lies ahead. This rebuilding process won't be easy, but you can emerge from the process as a stronger, more confident person, and that's a truth about the recovery process that you can look forward to as you embark on the journey ahead.

Conclusion

If I could sum up all the points in this chapter, I'd put it this way: Don't beat yourself up today for things you didn't know earlier about yourself, your abuser, and your past abusive relationship. People almost always act in the best way they can based on the best knowledge they have at any given point in time. Give yourself lots of grace and understanding as you look back on your past experiences with abuse, and know you were doing your best to manage your experiences at that time. Hindsight is always 20/20, so today as you look back on your abusive relationship, it's likely you now have a lot more clarity about your experiences than you had at the time. Allow the new knowledge you build over time to help you feel better about where you're going today, and not to feel worse about where you were in the past.

With that mindset, know that your efforts to continue educating yourself about abuse can continue as long as it's helpful to do so. Use new knowledge to develop greater self-awareness, but also as a powerful tool for helping others, as we'll discuss later in this book. There are many ways to continue your learning, such as through reading books, connecting with credible websites and social media channels, and taking classes or training programs through local, state, and national advocacy organizations. There's always so much to learn, and new knowledge will be coming out all the time, especially as researchers and practitioners work to understand emerging topics about abuse, such as technology-facilitated abuse and the mind-body connections to trauma. Personally, I've been studying this topic for almost 20 years now, and I feel like I'm still starting to scratch the surface about this important topic. With each new nugget of knowledge we gain, we become better equipped to understand our own experiences of abuse, as well as to help offer inspiration and support to others.

References

1. Murray, C. (2020). *In the Words of Survivors: The Importance of Education about Domestic Violence.* Retrieved April 17, 2020, from www.seethetriumph.org/blog/this-october-educate-yourself-and-others-about-domestic-violence.
2. Smith, S.G., Zhang, X., Basile, K.C., Merrick, M.T., Wang, J., Kresnow, M., Chen, J. (2018). *The National Intimate Partner and Sexual Violence Survey (NISVS): 2015 Data Brief – Updated Release.* Atlanta, GA: National Center for Injury Prevention and Control, Centers for Disease Control and Prevention. Retrieved July 5, 2020, from www.cdc.gov/violenceprevention/datasources/nisvs/summaryreports.html.
3. Murray, C. E., Crowe, A., & Flasch, P. (2015). Turning points: Critical incidents in survivors' decisions to end abusive relationships. *The Family Journal, 23,* 228–238. DOI: 10.1177/1066480715573705

5

TAKING BACK CONTROL OF YOUR MIND

"Overcoming abuse is when you're able to completely realize he was the one with the problem, not me. To allow oneself to live freely without fear of another person. To create yourself and completely release yourself from things that were pounded in your head day by day. To finally come to the point where you see that you deserve so much better. To make up one's mind that no matter how hard surviving is, just to keep on going because you know this is the only way to be safe, happy, and free. To allow yourself to live in the present rather than dwelling on the past. To come to the point where you accept there is still pain related to what happened, and that it's okay to love him, but it's not okay to be anyone's doormat. That returning to your abuser is no longer an option. To become strong willed and confident in your abilities. Knowing full heartedly that you truly are doing everything in your power to be the person you want to be. Coming to the point where you realize being loved is not being controlled but rather being free to be yourself."

~ Domestic Violence Survivor

As we discussed in the last chapter, abusive relationships are defined by their power and control dynamics. Abusers use many power and control tactics to manipulate their partners, and there's a large mental component to this control. In this chapter, we'll cover the cognitive dimensions of abuse and strategies to overcome this cognitive control. By cognitive dimensions, I'm referring to thought processes and patterns of thinking that can result from being subjected to an abusive partner's control. These cognitive dimensions are related to mental and emotional health, but we'll address those topics separately in Chapter 6.

In the current chapter, I'll share ways you can gain more awareness of how your thinking may have been impacted by your abuser's words and actions, as well as strategies for overcoming faulty belief systems you may have internalized as a result of your experiences with abuse. It can take a long time to work through the cognitive dimensions of abuse, and this is especially true if you have to continue to have some form of contact with your former abuser, such as if you share custody of children. Abusers can be relentless in the extent to which they try to manipulate, trick, and control the mind of their partners—and this often doesn't stop just because the romantic relationship ended.

Why and How Do Abusers Try to Control Your Mind?

There are many possible motives that drive abusers in their actions. Despite common patterns in abusive partners and relationships, every person is unique, so the exact drivers behind any individual abuser's actions are unique as well. In many cases, you'll never know or be able to figure out exactly what was going on in your abuser's mind that drove them to act in cruel and hurtful ways toward you. However, common characteristics of abusive partners include the following: untreated mental health, substance abuse, and/or personality disorders; untreated past trauma or victimization; internalized stereotypes or messages about relationships and gender roles; deep-seated insecurities; and learned behaviors in response to anger. *Regardless of what drives their actions, abusers are always fully responsible for their abusive actions, and none of these characteristics or motivations are excuses for their violent behavior.*

That said, taking time to reflect on what may have driven your abuser's behaviors might offer insights into the nature of the tactics they used to try and control your thought processes. If you decide to give this some thought, keep in mind it's likely you'll never fully understand what was going on in their mind. There are some people whose minds can never be understood, especially if you as a logical, rational person are trying to understand the mind of a person who is illogical and irrational. It's wise to only even consider trying to understand the mind of your abuser if doing so would help you understand your own experiences of the abuse—as well as if understanding your abuser's patterns could help you navigate any future interactions with them.

Whatever unique motivation your abuser had, perhaps the more important thing to remember during your healing journey is that abusers often use mind control as a way to get you to enter the relationship, keep you in the relationship, and establish and maintain control over you. Of course, abusers can't totally overtake every aspect of the inner workings of your mind, although some of them certainly can be very effective at brainwashing their partners. Abusers seem to understand that if they can get you to start questioning your own reality and doubting yourself, they'll be more likely to get you to stay with them and forgive them for abusive actions. The more they were able to influence your mind and thought processes, the more they were able to control your actions and responses to them.

Mental control takes many forms in abusive relationships. It can include gaslighting (i.e., trying to make you question your own reality), manipulation, criticism, verbal abuse, dishonesty, blaming you for things that weren't in your control, confusion, and constantly painting you as being the "bad guy," overly sensitive, or irrational. In your recovery process, it's much more important to focus on understanding the ways that your abuser tried to control your mind and how this impacted you, than it is to try and figure out what your abuser was thinking.

In my own recovery journey, it's been helpful to look back on things my abuser said or did to identify the extent of the pattern of the manipulation that I experienced, and how this led to my confusion during the relationship. This helped me understand many of my thoughts, emotions, and decisions that I experienced during the relationship. Before I really understood the pattern of manipulation, I questioned why I made certain decisions or "let him" treat me in certain ways. But as I looked back with greater understanding of the ways abusive partners exert mental control—and specifically the way my abuser used manipulation to influence my thinking—I gained greater self-awareness and was able to have more peace with my past experiences. To this day, I know I'll never fully understand why my abuser acted how he did—but understanding how his actions impacted my thinking has been a valuable part of my healing process.

Deciding to Take Back Control of Your Mind

One of the most powerful realizations many survivors have after leaving an abusive relationship is this: "My abuser doesn't control me anymore."

However, it's certainly possible to have physical freedom from a former abusive partner, but still have your mind be under the control of the lingering effects of your abuser's manipulation and psychological abuse. Overcoming the cognitive effects of abuse can be one of the more complicated aspects of the recovery process for many reasons, including the extent to which you internalized those beliefs, the potential added influence of other past trauma, and the ever-present nature of your thoughts.

We all have a pretty steady flow of thinking processes that is constantly running in the background of our minds. Sometimes, we have full awareness of these thoughts, such as when we're lying in bed and unable to sleep at night. Other times, however, we aren't fully aware of our thought processes and how they're impacting us in the present moment. Therefore, it's possible to be holding on to negative belief systems and harmful thought processes without even fully recognizing the extent to which they're impacting our lives. This is why it's critically important to be intentional and proactive about working on the mental dimensions of the abuse recovery process. Without identifying, challenging, and replacing negative thought processes, it's possible to carry them around for a long time and into many different areas of your life, including your parenting, career, friendships, and future romantic relationships.

Self-reflection: Internalized Messages Resulting from the Abuse

Deciding you want to work on taking back control of your mind is an important step in the recovery process. Even after making this decision, however, reclaiming your thought patterns can take time. Bring patience to this process, and know that seemingly smaller steps in the process can become the foundation for larger, more significant progress. An important first step in the process is examining (1) things your abuser said and did and (2) how you processed and internalized the messages that were communicated through your abuser's words and actions. Table 5.1 includes examples of possible messages that abusers convey, and then a corresponding thought or belief a survivor may internalize from those messages.

Did any of the messages or internalized beliefs resonate with you? Whether you could relate to the ones listed or there were other messages that were more impactful for you, it's a good idea to reflect on how your abuser's words and feelings influenced your thinking patterns. This could be a useful prompt for journaling or talking with a trusted friend or professional.

Table 5.1

Message in an Abuser's Words or Actions	Possible Survivor's Internalized Belief
You're at fault for how I acted.	The abuse was my fault.
You deserved it.	I deserve to be treated badly.
You'd be nothing without me.	I can't make it on my own.
There's something wrong with you.	I'm damaged or defective.
Nobody else would want to be with you.	I'll never find another relationship.
Nobody likes you.	I'm not likeable. Other people don't care about me.
You're such a failure.	I can't succeed (such as at work or at school).
Your dreams are stupid.	I should stop dreaming of a better future.
You're crazy.	There's something wrong with my mind.
You are a terrible parent.	I can't manage the demands of parenting.
You're too sensitive.	I overreact. My feelings don't matter.

When we look at the list of possible internalized beliefs that may result from abusers' mind games, it's hard to understand how such false beliefs could become deeply internalized into a survivor's thought processes. Keep in mind that abusive relationships typically involve lengthy patterns that repeat over and over again throughout a long period of time. It's one thing to be able to resist internalizing a false message when somebody conveys that message once, but when the message is delivered many times over the course of the relationship, those harmful messages can seep deeply into a person's thought processes and belief systems.

Also, abusers often convey the same message in many different ways. For example, if one of the messages your abuser conveyed to you was, "You're too sensitive," it's likely this was something they said to you directly on one or more occasions. However, they also likely conveyed the same message in other direct and subtle ways, such as by acting defensively if you shared your reactions to a hurtful thing they said or did, ridiculing you for crying or getting upset, or simply ignoring your request to talk about concerns you had about your relationship. In words and actions, these responses by your abuser likely led you to question if you really were being too sensitive, and then eventually giving in to the message because it was too taxing to continue to challenge it.

By the time survivors are freed from an abusive relationship, it's understandable if they've internalized a number of negative beliefs about themselves as a result of the abuse. Often, by the time the relationship ends, survivors have already begun to realize that many things their abusers said about them weren't true. Even then, unlearning harmful beliefs and replacing them with truthful, more positive belief systems can take time and effort. This is especially true if negative messages were reinforced by things other people have said or done to you as well, such as if you faced abuse in your family-of-origin.

Deciding to begin working to take back control of your mind as part of your recovery process is important for many reasons. Faulty, harmful beliefs can impact your life, whether you acknowledge them or not. Underlying belief systems drive many of our behaviors and our ways of interacting with the people and world around us. When we operate out of unexamined, faulty belief systems, our ability to experience health and wellbeing in many areas of life is limited. In addition to impacting your current functioning, negative belief systems also can limit your ability to make progress toward your future dreams and goals as well. That's why working toward freeing yourself from unhelpful belief systems is such a critical part of the recovery process. These underlying beliefs also can be an underlying factor in many of the emotional and mental health considerations we'll address in the next chapter.

Overcoming Self-Imposed Limiting Beliefs

In addition to considering negative belief systems that relate directly to the messages that your abuser communicated to you it's also important to note that some limiting belief systems and thought processes can be self-imposed. Whether or not you can trace these self-limiting beliefs back to your experiences with your abuser, these beliefs can add pressure and impose limitations that could hinder your healing process. Of course, healing from an abusive relationship *is* a daunting process. But, how you view that process—and your ability to work through it—plays a large role in how you experience the healing journey, and especially how you persist during the difficult time.

Here are some possible self-limiting beliefs that are natural for survivors to hold:

- I should just get over this.
- I should be feeling better by now.
- I'm too afraid/weak/damaged to take the next step toward a positive future.
- I can't trust anyone.
- I can't trust myself.

- This process is too hard.
- It's too late for me. I've missed my chance at a happy life.

Self-limiting beliefs are just as important to address as beliefs that were imposed by your abuser because they present a huge internal barrier to your healing journey. Because our belief systems drive our choices and behaviors, operating from limiting beliefs restricts our choices and behaviors and can lead us to rule out opportunities for positive change. In the next section, we'll focus on how to begin working to correct faulty belief systems. Because most of our focus in that section will be on internalized messages and thought processes stemming from the abuse, let's go ahead and consider alternative beliefs that can serve as replacements for the self-limiting beliefs listed above:

Table 5.2

Self-Limiting Belief	Possible Positive Alternative
I should just get over this.	Recovering from past abuse is a process that takes time and effort.
I should be feeling better by now.	There's no timeline for recovering from past abuse. I can take the time I need to heal.
I'm too afraid/weak/damaged to take the next step toward a positive future.	I'm strong. I can handle this next step and reach out for help along the way.
I can't trust anyone.	I can have good boundaries in place to help me let supportive people gain my trust and to help me keep unsupportive people at a safe distance.
I can't trust myself.	I have a powerful sense of intuition that I can rely on to guide my choices.
This process is too hard.	This process is hard, but I can make it by focusing on one small step at a time.
It's too late for me. I've missed my chance at a happy life.	I still deserve a happy, meaningful life.

Empowering beliefs like the ones listed in Table 5.2 can be important reminders as you face challenges—internal and external—throughout your healing journey. You can use these as replacements for negative thoughts, as we'll discuss in the next section, but you also can use these proactively and preventively by using them as mantras to repeat to yourself throughout your day. You may find it helpful to write notes with these positive messages in visible places throughout your home, such as on your mirror, beside your desk, or on your refrigerator. These visible reminders can help reinforce the positive beliefs you're working to build internally.

Correcting Faulty Belief Systems

Negative belief systems and thought processes can become deeply ingrained, so changing them is a challenging process. You may find it helpful to work with a professional counselor who specializes in Cognitive-Behavioral Therapy to help you with this process, and I'll share suggestions for finding a counselor in the next chapter. Below, I'll outline the basic steps in the process of transforming negative, faulty belief systems into more corrective, positive beliefs. To illustrate the steps, we'll look at the example of an abuser's message, "Nobody likes you," which may be internalized as a survivor's belief, "I'm not likeable. Other people don't care about me."

Step 1: Identifying Negative, Faulty Beliefs and Thought Processes

Hopefully, you've already begun this step as you've read through the first parts of this chapter. If you didn't do so earlier, take some time to identify messages your abuser conveyed and how you internalized those into negative beliefs, as well as the self-limiting beliefs that you may be holding onto. This step has two levels. First, identify general patterns of negative, faulty beliefs that impact your overall views about yourself and your life, such as by reflecting on or journaling about these beliefs. The second level can be a bit more complicated, and that is learning to identify these types of beliefs in the moment, as they arise in the middle of different circumstances in your daily life.

Recognizing negative, faulty beliefs in the moment is difficult because the amount of time between your thoughts, feelings, and actions can be very short, so you may not even notice when negative thought processes are driving your feelings and actions. For example, in our example of an internalized belief of "I'm not likeable," imagine you're out in the grocery store and see a casual, but usually very friendly, acquaintance on the other side of the store. If you believe you're not likeable, you may avoid the acquaintance and try to avoid seeing them because you think they don't like you. However, if you held a positive belief that you *are* likeable, you may instead go over for a brief visit with your acquaintance and enjoy the chance to have a friendly chat. Even if you're in a hurry, your belief that you're likeable will help you know you can have boundaries to keep the conversation short, but you won't worry later that the other person won't like you anymore since you had to rush off.

Because the moments between thoughts and reactions can be so brief, it's helpful to develop quick ways to check in with yourself to gain awareness about your thought processes and how they impact your behaviors. In the example above, it could be as simple as noticing an initial sense of anxiety that comes up when you see your acquaintance, and pausing for a moment to ask yourself, "What about this situation is causing my anxiety?" Answering that question could help you identify whether you're experiencing the tension because you're afraid saying hello will make you late, or if it's something deeper like a fear that the other person wouldn't want to talk to you.

Learning to identify negative, faulty beliefs is a crucial first step in the process of building a more positive, accurate belief system. Because these beliefs often go unchecked, it's wise to reflect on them from the big picture view, as well as to become more aware of them in the moment.

Step 2: Externalizing Negative, Faulty Beliefs

Once you've identified a faulty belief, another helpful step is to move them out of your mind and into some other external format. Of course, this "external" format could be just a more intentional thought that you move from the background into the forefront of your mind. However, if possible, it's helpful to actually physically move these thoughts out of your mind and write them out on a piece of paper or some secure electronic platform, such as in a note on your phone or in a document on your computer. There's something powerful about seeing a negative thought on paper, as this can help you see more clearly the negative nature of the belief.

When you see the words on paper, ask yourself if you'd say those words to your best friend. Many people are much kinder to other people than they are to themselves in their minds. As you start to get negative, faulty beliefs out of your mind and into a visible format you can see, recognize the possible source of these beliefs (such as if they're directly related to something your abuser said or did to you), and remind yourself you can question whether they are true. Just because you think something in your mind doesn't necessarily mean that it's true. If you're a visual person, you might even imagine holding your thought in your hands and giving yourself permission to look at it from different angles so you'll feel more comfortable challenging it when you move to the next step.

Going back to our example, at this point a person holding the belief might take some time to sit down and write out the following: "I have a belief that

I'm not likeable. I have a belief that other people don't care about me." Here, even the wording of "I have a belief…" compared to "I believe…" starts to help separate the person from the belief to make it easier to move forward to challenging and eventually replacing that belief with a more positive alternative.

Step 3: Putting Negative, Faulty Beliefs to the Test

Once you've identified and externalized a negative, faulty belief, it's time to start to question the belief and challenge its truthfulness. Three questions to help with this testing process are listed below, along with sample answers in response to the example belief that "I'm not likeable":

- *How and where did I come to believe this?* In the example of believing you're not likeable and other people don't care about you, you might be able to trace that back to comments your abuser made about you, but it's also possible you held this belief earlier in life as a result of other experiences in your family or childhood, such as having been bullied in school. Recognizing the source of a negative belief can help you identify how these beliefs are based in specific experiences or interactions with others and don't reflect the full depth of who you are as a person.
- *Is there any evidence to support this?* Most likely, you could find some evidence to both support and refute a negative thought or belief. Of course, not everyone you meet will like you, for example, so you could count that as evidence to support the belief. However, most likely, as you dig deeper into exploring whether there's evidence to support a faulty belief, you'll find that the overwhelming amount of evidence does not support the belief, and in fact, you can probably find a lot of evidence to support the truth of an alternative belief. In the case of a belief about not being likeable, you can probably identify a lot of positive qualities in yourself that would be appealing to other people, and you probably can identify a number of people you've known over time who have truly cared for you. As the evidence begins to grow for the truth of a more positive, alternative belief, you'll feel more confident in leaving the unhelpful belief systems behind.
- *How is this belief over-simplified and not reflective of the complexity of real life?* Life is complicated, and our thoughts can become oversimplified and not reflect the real complexity of life. For example, if we're questioning our belief, "I'm not likeable. Other people don't care about me," we need to start digging deeper to challenge the faulty assumptions that allow

negative beliefs to exist. In this case, some questions I would consider asking include the following: Who gets to decide what makes a person likeable? Who said that it's important to be likeable to everyone? Isn't it okay to have people close to me who like me, but understand that there will be others who don't like me? And, even if other people don't care about me, why should I assume their lack of caring has anything to do with me and isn't a reflection of their own character? By asking this sort of question, you can take important steps toward defining what's most important to you in life. You may even find by asking yourself questions like these that you come up with entirely different ways of thinking about your life. In this case, a survivor following this line of questioning may eventually find themself concluding: "I get to decide if I like myself, and I can find people who also like those things about me and will care about me. I don't have to worry what everyone around me thinks after all."

Step 4: Learning to Use Positive Self-talk

Be more intentional about the process of developing positive thoughts and beliefs within your inner dialogue. Again, positive self-talk can be done both in response to negative thoughts and beliefs, as well as more proactively by reminding yourself of positive statements throughout your day. It can be helpful to come up with positive affirmations to repeat to yourself on a regular basis. Even just one or two statements can be helpful, especially if they're meaningful to you and easy to remember. For example, you might say, "I've got this," or "I'm getting stronger every day." Some people feel silly or cheesy with this sort of thing, but keep in mind that short slogans can be very powerful. Remember that many companies spend millions of dollars coming up with the right slogan to keep their company at the top of consumers' minds. You can harness this same power—without the same big price tag—to keep your own goal of reclaiming control of your mind at the top of your mind.

Turning back to our example, "I'm not likeable. Other people don't care about me," here are a few examples of positive self-talk statements that could replace those faulty beliefs:

> "I'm a good person who's getting even better every day."
> "The right people I want in my life will like and care for me."
> "I deserve to have a solid group of loved ones who care for me."
> "No matter what other people do, I can care for myself."

Practicing positive self-talk can feel unnatural at first, but with practice, it becomes easier and more comfortable. Even when it feels silly, it can be a powerful tool for helping to replace unhelpful beliefs with more positive, helpful ones.

Step 5: Intentionally Developing More Positive Underlying Belief Systems

It's important progress to replace individual negative thoughts, but even deeper progress can be made when you build more positive, comprehensive thought patterns and belief systems. Think about the difference between being a "glass half full" or a "glass half empty" type of person. Of course, people tend to be more optimistic or pessimistic as part of their overall personality, but there are certainly changeable parts of people's thought patterns that can help them become more resilient and positive in their ways of thinking, even if they don't fully ever embrace a life of wearing rose-colored glasses.

If you've been abused, it's understandable to have developed negative ways of thinking as a result of those experiences. As part of your recovery process, you can build new ways of viewing yourself, other people, and the world around you. This takes time and effort, but it is possible and becomes easier the further along you move in your recovery process. Be intentional about developing more positive underlying belief systems, and be creative in how you do this.

For example, a survivor who has a set of beliefs around the thought, "I'm not likeable. Other people don't care about me," might also have some of the following related beliefs: "I'm not smart. I'm boring. I'll probably always be alone. Other people can't be trusted. And, I'll always be stuck in this bad situation." Within these beliefs, we can see a pattern of self-isolation and a tendency to interpret things in a negative light. If that survivor was interested in building a more positive belief system framework, the following actions might be helpful: (1) developing a set of positive affirmations to repeat on a daily basis; (2) posting positive quotes and images in visible places around the house, (3) reading books and listening to podcasts that focus on personal development, (4) surrounding oneself with positive, supportive, and trustworthy people, (5) developing playlists with uplifting music, and (6) exploring spiritual beliefs and practices.

There's a lot of negativity in the world today, and it's not possible to totally avoid this. Building more positive cognitive frameworks isn't about ignoring problems and pretending everything is okay all the time. Instead, this type of positive thinking allows for negative thoughts, feelings, and experiences to be acknowledged and addressed, while also intentionally fostering an internal and external environment that supports our future growth, honors our personal strengths, and supports our resilience, even during difficult times.

Step 6: Practicing Until New Patterns of Thinking Become Natural

When you've faced the onslaught of negative words and actions from an abuser, negative thinking patterns can come to feel normal since you were living for so long in a negative, high-anxiety situation. You may not be used to building yourself up, let alone having other people in your life help build you up as well. The process of overcoming negative, faulty beliefs and thought patterns can take time. You may even feel more uncomfortable when you first start using positive thought processes than you felt with negative thoughts, just because it's new and unfamiliar.

Think about this process of retraining your mind like the process of retraining your body through exercise. If you were going to start lifting weights at the gym for the first time (or the first time in a while), your body would probably feel uncomfortable while you're lifting weights, as well as sore in the days after your workout. Over time and with consistent practice, you'll be able to comfortably lift the same amount of weight that used to make you uncomfortable and sore. Training your mind is similar—it can feel uncomfortable and awkward in the beginning, but in time, new patterns of thinking can take root and become natural, normal ways of thinking.

If we think back to the example of the person in the grocery store who believes they're not likeable, imagine we could fast forward that scenario after several months of time in which the survivor was practicing new ways of thinking and positive self-talk. If that survivor were to run into an acquaintance in the grocery store after all of this hard work, it's possible they wouldn't even think twice about approaching the other person to say hello—or if they did, it would be more about a concern about running late to another commitment than any level of fear of not being liked by the other person. Over time, positive ways of thinking that once seemed strange and unfamiliar become natural. These new, natural ways of thinking can help support their further growth in many other areas of life.

Conclusion

Your mind is one of your most powerful tools to support your healing journey. Look no further than your abuser's intense focus on controlling your mind to understand the importance of taking back that control as you move forward on your healing journey. Your abuser understood that if they could control your ways of thinking, they could control your actions and responses to their actions. One of the most powerful decisions you can make during your recovery process is to reclaim your right to control your thoughts and belief patterns. Overcoming negative internalized messages that resulted from abuse is no easy feat! However, your efforts to do so can help you make positive changes in virtually every other aspect of your recovery. For example, if you can shape your belief system to gain confidence in your ability to be a good parent, you'll be better equipped to navigate parenting stress. Relatedly, if you believe you have the power to be successful in your career and that you still have plenty of time to strive toward meaningful educational and career goals, you can strengthen your courage to pursue those goals and overcome challenges along the way. By taking back your right to have control over your thought processes, your mind can become one of your most important resources to help you move forward in your journey to triumph over past abuse.

6

FOSTERING POSITIVE MENTAL AND EMOTIONAL HEALTH

"During those 'dark' days, I had people comment to me that I seemed unhappy, that I never smiled. I didn't. I felt like I was drowning and had no means to pull myself out of the water to get to dry land and help. I was ashamed, lonely and felt totally helpless. However, I have come through the darkness and now have a contented and fulfilled life. I have a greater empathy for those in similar circumstances and take joy in helping others see the light at the end of the tunnel. I am happy and frequently and openly laugh! I am no longer that shell of a woman that I once was, and life is good!"

~ Domestic Violence Survivor

In addition to reclaiming control of your thoughts and belief systems, an important aspect of triumphing over abuse is healing from mental and emotional health consequences of abuse. Mental and emotional health overlap with the thought processes we addressed in the last chapter. However, the thinking patterns we covered in Chapter 5 relate to the *content* of your thoughts, and in this chapter, we'll look more at the *processes* involved in how your mind and emotions work. In other words, the cognitive dimensions we covered in the previous chapter addressed *what* you think, and mental and emotional health concerns reflect *how* you think and feel.

It's normal to experience mental health and emotional health challenges in the aftermath of an abusive relationship. Your mental and emotional health are important to your recovery process and to the overall quality of your life. Your health and wellbeing in these areas have a major influence on your behaviors and choices. In addition, chronic, untreated mental or emotional health symptoms can contribute to impaired physical health and hindered functioning in your relationships and career. Ongoing mental and emotional health challenges impact your energy levels and motivation for making positive changes in your life and for persevering when life is difficult.

In this chapter, we'll explore the links between experiencing the trauma of abuse and the risk for mental and emotional health challenges. Then, we'll focus on ways to seek professional support from a counselor or therapist to help navigate these challenges. As we'll discuss later, many professional counselors and therapists lack basic training on the dynamics of abusive relationships. Therefore, I'll share tips for finding a counselor who has the training and understanding needed to offer appropriate support to survivors.

The Trauma of Abuse

For most people, experiencing an abusive relationship can be considered a traumatic experience. The United States Substance Abuse and Mental Health Services Administration (SAMHSA) defines trauma as "an event, series of events, or set of circumstances that is experienced by an individual as physically or emotionally harmful or life threatening and that has lasting adverse effects on the individual's functioning and mental, physical, social, emotional, or spiritual well-being."[1] Professionals sometimes refer to this definition of trauma as "The 3 E's," referring to the following three key words in the definition: event(s), experienced, and effects. In line with these three terms, it's easy to see how abuse can be considered traumatic. First, abuse may include one significant event, but usually involves patterns of power and control and abuse tactics that we discussed earlier in this book. Second, abuse usually is experienced as bringing real or threatened harm to people who are victimized. Third, survivors often face negative consequences in their lives that result directly and indirectly from the abuse they experienced.

Understanding links between trauma and mental health is important because traumatic events can contribute to traumatic stress, and this traumatic stress can contribute to mental health symptoms, such as depression and anxiety, as well as difficult managing emotions. Another reason it's wise to understand the nature of trauma is because it can help you understand your reactions to the abuse you suffered. Traumatic events aren't the same as normal, day-to-day events. They're outside of the ordinary challenges and stressors of daily life. Traumatic events can include things like natural disasters (e.g., hurricanes or tornadoes), car accidents, and the sudden death of a loved one, as well as abuse.

Traumatic experiences are exceptionally challenging, and they place extreme burdens on our coping resources. Think about how someone might react if their house had just been destroyed in a tornado. How would you expect them to react? You wouldn't expect them to shrug it off and say, "No big deal," would you? Of course not—you'd expect they'd be extremely distressed, crying, and in deep emotional pain over such a tremendous loss. In fact, you'd probably be more concerned about someone whose house was just destroyed in a tornado if they didn't show signs of distress. You might even think they were in denial or lying!

Traumatic experiences place a heavy burden on a person's ability to cope and manage their emotions. They are *unusual events* that call for *unusual responses*. These events can push even the most mentally and emotionally healthy person to the edge of their normal levels of functioning. Why is it, then, that we should be surprised or place added stigma on survivors of the trauma of abuse when they experience mental or emotional health symptoms? This includes self-imposed stigma and shame—even many survivors themselves fall into the belief that they should just "snap out of it" and move on. Instead of wishing away the mental and emotional health consequences of abuse, it's much more helpful to acknowledge that these consequences are natural, expected reactions to facing the unnatural, unexpected trauma of abuse. Acknowledging lingering mental and emotional health effects of the abuse is an important first step toward being able to map out a plan to process them and move toward a more positive level of mental and emotional functioning.

Let's take a closer look at the possible mental health and emotional health effects of abuse, and starting with the emotional aspects.

Emotional Effects of Past Abuse

It's helpful to think about the emotional effects of past abuse at two levels. First, we can consider the immediate emotional states you experience. And second, we can look at the bigger picture of how well overall you're able to manage and express emotions. The first level looks at the question of, "How am I feeling in any given moment?" The second level considers the question, "How are my overall emotional management and regulation abilities?" Both levels are important to understand throughout the long-term process of recovering from past abuse.

Immediate Emotional States

In any given moment, you might be experiencing any number of possible feelings and emotions. This could include happiness, sadness, anger, frustration, joy, peacefulness, irritation, or fear, among many other possibilities. This is true for all people, whether or not they've experienced abuse. Feelings and emotions are a normal part of life, although this can be a difficult thing to understand for people with a history of being made to feel ashamed or weak when they expressed feelings. Often, life with an abusive partner involves pressure to minimize or deny your feelings. Abusers may make clear they don't care how their partners feel, and this can lead victims and survivors into a pattern of denying their feelings. Pushing down emotions can become a survival technique over the course of an abusive relationship, so the recovery process often involves being intentional about learning to experience and express emotions again.

Emotions can be very intense throughout the recovery process, and especially very early on in that process. In one moment, you might be feeling at peace and confident in your decisions and current situation, and then in the very next moment, something might come up internally or externally that sends you into a negative spiral of emotions. In fact, there may be times when you feel flooded by emotions, almost to the point of being totally overwhelmed by them. This is one of the reasons we discussed earlier the critical importance of building your coping resources as one of the first steps in the recovery process. It's important to have strategies available to navigate these intense emotions as they arise.

Early in my own process of recovering from my abusive relationship, I remember feeling like I was on an emotional roller coaster. This roller coaster had many high highs, such as when I felt elated I was finally free from my abuser, as well as many very low lows, such as when I was overcome by sadness or anger when I thought back on specific incidents of abuse. My mantra for making it through this emotional roller coaster was, "Ride the wave." I reminded myself of this mantra as one way to give myself permission to feel whatever emotions came up at any moment and avoid pushing away those emotions so I could work through them instead.

Emotional highs and lows are common for all people, but especially for survivors, and even more as you're just beginning your recovery process. However, there's no set timeline for emotions, and sometimes survivors push emotions to the side in the immediate aftermath of abuse because they're focusing on practical things and operating in survival mode. Intense emotions can arise at different points of the recovery process, not just in the beginning. To some extent, experiencing emotions is a sign of progress in recovery, although admittedly sometimes this progress is painful.

Begin to pay greater attention to your emotions as you go throughout your recovery journey, and give yourself permission to feel emotions as they arise, but do so in a way that feels safe and comfortable for you. It's okay if sometimes you need to set aside emotions and process them later when the timing is right. The important thing is to process them at some point and in a way that makes sense to you. Unexpressed and unprocessed emotions can build up over time and come out in unhealthy ways, such as through extreme stress, mental health symptoms, or emotional outbursts toward friends and family.

If you feel like you're on an emotional roller coaster as you move through different parts of your recovery process, plan for how to best respond to the ups, downs, and in-betweens in your feelings. Remind yourself that your feelings are a sign your heart and your head are working to try and make sense of a very unnatural, difficult experience. Know that you are justified in feeling any feelings that you have. But also, know that your feelings are temporary, and they may or may not reflect the truth of a situation. For example, you may feel extreme sadness and hopelessness because you feel like you will never find a loving relationship again. The feelings you're feeling are real, but the thoughts behind them may not be true. Work toward honoring your feelings (e.g., "It's okay to feel sad and hopeless right now"), while also giving yourself permission to think critically about the thoughts underlying the feelings (e.g., "Just because I feel sad, doesn't mean that it's true I won't find love again").

Overall Emotional Management

As you become more aware of how you're feeling at any given moment, it's also important to take a bigger picture look at your overall capacity to manage and respond to emotions in constructive ways. This will help you honor and express your emotions, and also identify when your emotional responses may be a signal of concern or a reason to seek additional help, such as from a counselor.

There may be some truth to the old adage that "Time heals all wounds." As more time passes since you faced abuse, you probably will notice some of the intensity of your emotions begins to fade. However, I'm sure we all can think of examples of people who weren't able to settle the hurts of their pasts, and they continued to remain bitter and stuck in a cycle of negativity long after those hurtful experiences ended. Perhaps you may even see yourself in that description, and if you do, try to acknowledge that insight without self-condemnation. It's never too late to work toward overcoming the past, and in fact that's what the whole journey we're covering in this book is all about: intentionally building your capacity to process, manage, and choose how you will respond to your emotions so you can handle the challenges of daily life and increase your freedom from hurts and emotional scars of the past.

You already probably have some positive emotional management resources at your disposal, especially if you focused on building up coping resources as we discussed early in this book. On the other hand, it's normal for survivors to have some lasting challenges with overall emotional management. Consider the extent to which your abuser's actions hindered your capacity to manage your emotions. Did your abuser make fun of you for expressing emotions, or call you too sensitive? Or, did they gaslight you into making your doubt and question your feelings? Abusers typically don't take their partners' feelings into consideration, and they may even have tried to forbid you from feeling, or at least expressing, your feelings.

In light of those possible experiences within your abusive relationship, it's likely you came out with some impacts to your emotional management abilities. This isn't because there's something wrong with you, and in fact it's likely an indicator of your ability to adapt to changing circumstances. Suppressing emotions during an abusive relationship is a way to manage emotions within the context of that relationship—it also probably was a way to help you stay safer from your partner's wrath. However, once you're out of that abusive context, continuing to suppress your feelings can hinder your recovery process and impact your relationships and emotional health.

Emotional recovery from past abuse is important for all of these reasons, and it involves building your capacity to experience and express emotions and developing your emotional intelligence and self-awareness. Below are suggestions for practical steps you can take to build your emotional management capacity.

Reflect on Your Typical Responses to Emotions

Set aside time for self-reflection on your patterns of responding to emotions. Consider how your emotional response patterns have changed over time, such as before you were in the abusive relationship, during the relationship, in the immediate aftermath of the relationship, and currently. Notice if there are consistent patterns in how you respond to emotions you experience as positive, negative, and neutral. Notice which emotions are easier and harder for you to feel and/or express. For example, you may notice you feel a lot of anger internally, but you have a difficult time expressing anger to others. For an even deeper dive, consider what you experienced and learned about emotions during your childhood and in your family-of-origin. Often, the roots of our patterns for responding to emotions can be found in messages we received very early in life.

Develop a System for Tracking Your Emotions and Responses

Once you've reflected on past experiences and patterns of responding to emotions, set up processes to continue your self-reflection into your emotional experiences. You may find it helpful to keep an emotions journal or using a mood-tracking app on your phone, or even set up calendar reminders to do a quick emotional self check-in a couple times a day. At this point, don't focus too much on changing anything in your ways of managing emotions, but focus more on gaining awareness of your patterns. For example, track what feelings you're having, when those feelings arise, what the precipitating events were, what you wanted to do in response to the emotion, and how you actually responded. Over time, tracking emotions in this way can offer valuable insights to identify ways you're managing your emotions well, as well as areas for growth.

Learn New Ways of Expressing Emotions

When you identify opportunities for growth in your emotional management patterns, commit to learning and applying new, constructive ways of responding to emotions to support your growth in those areas. Seeking help from a professional counselor can be one way to do this, and we'll cover tips for finding a counselor later in this chapter. Other ways of learning new emotional management skills include reading books and credible online resources on the subject, participating in psychoeducational workshops, and doing personal experimentation to find out which strategies work best for you.

Lean into Your Support Network

Seek support from trusted friends and family members as you work on building your emotional management abilities. This is helpful because changing patterns can be difficult, and having supportive people on your side can offer both practical and moral support. Practically speaking, supportive people can help you practice new ways of expressing emotions, such as by doing role plays of emotionally-intense situations. They also can offer constructive feedback and help you brainstorm ideas for other ways to handle difficult emotions. In addition, the moral support you receive from others who are there to cheer you on and share their own challenges with managing emotions can be invaluable as you navigate this difficult part of the abuse recovery process.

Identify Specific Emotions that Are Especially Challenging for You

Chances are, there are some emotions that are more difficult for you to express than others. For some people, it can be difficult to express positive emotions like love and affection, especially if past expressions of these emotions were met with abuse. For others, emotions like anger or frustration can feel scary to express, so they may try to bury these emotions. As you increase your emotional awareness, pay special attention to emotional responses that are especially difficult for you, and make extra efforts to increase your ability to respond to these emotions in ways that feel safe and comfortable for you.

Practice, Practice, Practice

Finally, it takes time and consistent effort to build our capacity for emotional management and regulation. Emotional response patterns can become deeply embedded within our psyche, so growth and change can take time. Don't get down on yourself if you experience what feel like setbacks along the way. These supposed setbacks can offer new insights into your overall progress and help you identify new areas for further growth. As you continue to practice healthier, more adaptive ways of responding to your emotions, you'll find these responses become more natural over time.

Mental Health Impacts of Abuse

Emotional health is closely related to mental health, and in this section, we'll move from looking at patterns of responding to emotions to more specific mental health concerns survivors may face. Before going any further, I want to emphasize the importance of seeking help from a qualified mental health professional if you're experiencing mental health symptoms or concerns. We'll cover tips for finding qualified mental health professionals at the end of this chapter. It's important to seek professional help for mental health concerns, just like it's important to seek help from a medical professional if you're facing a physical illness or injury. Of course, if you faced physical health impacts of abuse, it's also wise to seek support for those concerns from a medical professional as well throughout your recovery process.

Avoid the temptation to diagnose or label yourself with mental health disorders. Diagnosis of mental health disorders should be done by qualified mental health professionals, just as diagnosis of physical conditions should be done by medical professionals. You can find a wealth of information about mental health conditions online, but it's important to seek help from a trained professional because self-diagnosis can be dangerous and inaccurate, and a professional clinical assessment is a key step in the overall process of treating mental health disorders. Trained professionals can help sort out symptoms from an actual diagnosis (e.g., differentiate between having a depressed mood and experiencing Major Depressive Disorder).

With all of these disclaimers aside, it's important for survivors to understand that mental health symptoms are common in the aftermath of the trauma of abuse, and this is part of why seeking professional support if you're facing symptoms is so important. Some of the more common mental health symptoms among survivors include posttraumatic stress, anxiety, and depression. Sometimes, these symptoms meet the criteria for a diagnosis, and sometimes, they don't. The most important consideration for survivors is the extent to which these symptoms impact your life and your recovery process. If you're facing any symptoms to an extent that they're causing you distress or impacting your ability to function in any areas of life, seek professional support to better understand these symptoms and learn ways to manage them.

Just as there can be a stigma surrounding experiencing abuse, there also can be a stigma attached to mental health symptoms and diagnoses. However, both of these layers of stigma are unwarranted, as there should be no shame attached to being abused or facing mental health challenges. In fact, it takes much courage and strength to live through both of these experiences. Don't let anyone make you feel ashamed or embarrassed by your experiences, and continue to seek the help you need to work toward building the healthy, meaningful life that you desire.

Seeking Professional Help for Mental and Emotional Health Effects of Abuse

Throughout this chapter, I've emphasized the importance of considering professional help to help navigate the mental and emotional health impacts of abuse. Although most of this section focuses on tips for seeking help from a mental health professional for counseling or psychotherapy, I'll add that a psychiatric or medical evaluation may be useful as well, especially if there's a chance psychiatric medications may be beneficial as part of your overall approach to managing mental health symptoms. When seeking any type of professional mental health support, try to find a professional who has adequate training, experience, and understanding in the areas of trauma and the dynamics of abuse. A professional who lacks this understanding may not be equipped to offer the support you need during your recovery process.

Unfortunately, it can be difficult to find mental health professionals who are competent to address abuse, although this is improving as more professionals are being trained in trauma-responsive approaches to therapy. Even with these advances in the field, far too many mental health professionals don't receive much training on domestic violence during their training in graduate school. This lack of training is a big problem for many reasons—including that counselors may not be aware of the full scope of safety-related issues that survivors often face. In addition, they also may not be prepared to address trauma-related symptoms that can result from experiences like abuse victimization. In our See the Triumph research, we heard from several survivors who experienced further stigmatization from mental health professionals who they turned to for help.

However, there are mental health professionals who have training and experience to help survivors with mental health, relationship, and other recovery-related concerns, both immediately after the abuse and in the long-term. If you're seeking counseling, talk with any prospective counselors to learn whether they know enough to be able to provide safe, effective services. The list of questions below[2] is useful to ask prospective counselors to learn their views toward and counseling approaches for working with survivors. In the list below, I use the term *counselor* to refer to any qualified mental health professional, which might include psychologists, clinical social workers, marriage and family therapists, and clinical mental health counselors. The questions below are designed to apply to professionals from different backgrounds, and it's possible to find a counselor that's a good fit from any of these professional disciplines.

- *What level of training do you have on the topic of intimate partner violence?* Ideally, the counselor will have taken a graduate-level course on family violence. Other coursework may have been taken at the undergraduate level. However, many training programs don't offer courses on this topic. If that's the case, ask if the counselor sought out continuing education courses on the dynamics of abuse. Counselors also may have done additional reading on the topic, such as through professional books and research-based journal articles.

- *How much experience have you had working with clients impacted by abuse?* If a counselor lacks extensive experience, they should be working with a clinical supervisor who's had sufficient experience in working with clients who've faced abuse. A counselor with experience should be able to describe their general approach to working with clients who've been abused.

- *Do you understand safety planning? How would you address safety planning when working with clients impacted by abuse?* Safety planning is a basic intervention for survivors of abusive relationships. Survivors may face safety risks, whether they're still in the abusive relationship, have just left, or even if they've been out of the abusive relationship for a long time. Therefore, it's important to ask a prospective counselor how they would account for safety concerns through the course of counseling.

- *Would you provide couple counseling when a couple is experiencing violence? If so, how would you proceed?* In general, conjoint couple counseling (i.e., when both partners are together in the session) is not recommended when couples are experiencing violence in their relationship. Couple counseling can create an unsafe situation for survivors, and it can imply that the survivor shared some blame for the abuse. There are some situations in which a counselor may make an exception to this general rule to avoid couple counseling when violence is present. However, you should ensure that a counselor you're seeing understands the safety risks inherent in doing so and would put in place a number of safeguards to protect the survivor.

- *Are you required to assign a diagnosis to all clients you counsel? If so, how do you account for trauma symptoms in your assessment and diagnosis?* A mental health disorder diagnosis may be required in order for a counselor to receive third-party (e.g., insurance) reimbursement for providing services. However, the application of a diagnosis of a mental health disorder label must be done carefully, as these labels can add increased stigma that a survivor may experience from others, as well as internally. Without a careful assessment, symptoms of the traumatic aspects of the abuse may be mislabeled through inappropriate diagnoses. Therefore, it's important for a counselor to understand how to account for trauma symptoms in the diagnosis process.

- *Are you familiar with community resources and legal processes related to abusive relationships?* An abusive relationship is not just a mental health issue—it has implications for many aspects of survivors' lives, including physical health, work and educational functioning, and parenting. In addition, abuse is often a crime, and survivors may be involved in the legal system in various ways (e.g., seeking protective orders or getting divorced). Therefore, it's important to work with a counselor who understands the broad range of resources available in your community so they can help you connect with other sources of support you may need.

If you're having a hard time finding a suitable counselor on your own, your local domestic violence agency may be able to provide you a list of counselors who they trust. In general, it's important to feel comfortable and safe with any counselor you choose to work with. When you're screening prospective counselors, if they say anything that makes you uncomfortable, pay attention to your intuition. That person may not be the right counselor for you. Although it can be difficult to find the right counselor for you, don't give up until you've found the person you believe is most likely to be able to help and support you.

Once you've found the right counselor, here are a few basic ideas for what you can expect from the therapy process. First, just as we discussed earlier in this book, counseling for survivors of abuse usually begins by focusing on building your coping resources before delving deeply into the details of the traumatic experiences you faced. As such, it may take a few sessions (or more) before you begin a deeper exploration of your experiences with abuse, although feel free to mention any topics you'd like to discuss with your counselor at any time. Your needs should drive the overall process of counseling, and the counselor should support you in identifying and addressing these needs.

One of the most frustrating—but also ultimately helpful—things about counseling is that a good counselor doesn't give you all the answers, but helps you discover the best answers to your concerns for yourself. This is frustrating because there may be times you wish your counselor would just tell you what to do, and this is especially true if you developed a sense of dependence on others and a lack of confidence in yourself as a result of abuse. However, although an effective counselor may offer you suggestions to consider and "assignments" to complete between counseling sessions, ultimately the counseling process will be most helpful if it empowers you to make decisions for yourself. Your counselor can further empower you by balancing validation and support on the one hand with gently challenging you to take calculated risks and grow on the other. In the abuse recovery process, counseling is likely to start with more validation and support. Over time, as your coping resources and strength are built up, your counselor may offer more gentle challenges to help you continue to grow.

In good counseling, professionals don't breed dependence in their clients, and ultimately their long-term goal should be to help you reach a point where you feel confident to manage life's challenges on your own. That said, it's valuable to keep the door open to return to counseling in the future, whether with the same counselor or a different one. Think about it like your relationship with your primary care doctor: There may be times when you're sick when you see them frequently, and then you may have only occasional check-ins while things are going well. Consider building in an annual (or quarterly, or whatever time frame makes sense to you) "checkup" with your counselor, or just identify a set of signs (e.g., feelings of extreme sadness that last for more than one week or having a hard time keeping up with demands at work) that suggest that you would benefit from reaching back out for added support.

Conclusion

Your mental and emotional health are important aspects of the overall quality of your life. As a survivor of past abuse, especially given the emotional repercussions of this abuse, it's likely you may be facing lasting effects of the abuse on your mental and emotional wellbeing. This is a natural and understandable response to the trauma of abuse. Be intentional about your emotional recovery process by increasing awareness of your feelings and emotions at any given point in time, as well as by developing your overall capacity to manage your emotions in a healthy way. Understand some of the common mental health impacts of past abuse, and be open to seeking assistance from a mental health professional to help you along the way.

References

1. Substance Abuse and Mental Health Services Administration (2020). *Trauma and Violence*. Retrieved June 28, 2020, from www.samhsa.gov/trauma-violence.
2. This list of questions is adapted from a See the Triumph blog post I wrote, *"Finding a Counselor Who is Competent To Serve Survivors,"* on January 6, 2014. www.seethetriumph. org/blog/finding-a-counselor-who-is-competent-to-serve-survivors.

7

BEING THE BEST PARENT YOU CAN BE

"I have come to a place of acceptance about my past and those who have hurt me. I no longer feel ashamed about what happened to me, but rather use it to fuel me to make a difference for others who are living through what I lived through. It means raising my children to know what healthy boundaries and relationships are so they can avoid relationships like the one they watched between me and their father. It means living with the lights on instead of hiding in dark corners."

~ Domestic Violence Survivor

Parenting is one of the most difficult jobs in life. If you are a parent and a survivor of abuse, it's likely your experiences with abuse will impact your parenting in some way. In our research related to See the Triumph, we've heard about many parenting-related challenges from the survivors who shared their stories with us. A common theme is that parenting challenges are especially difficult because they cut right to your heart when they impact your children, who are almost certainly among the people you love most in the world.

This chapter walks through several aspects of parenting challenges faced by survivors. Depending on your situation, some of these challenges may be more or less relevant to your life. So, as with all aspects of this book, focus on what applies to your life, and you can view the other aspects of parenting we'll discuss as educational about what others may go through, even if it doesn't apply directly to your life. There are four main topics we'll cover. First, we'll look at how parenting stress in general can be challenging for people with a history of the trauma of abuse. Second, we'll discuss considerations for talking with children of different ages about abuse. The third topic is an especially complex and challenging one: attempting to co-parent with your former abuser. Finally, we'll cover special considerations for survivors who face abuse and ongoing challenges related to child custody and family court issues.

Parenting in the Aftermath of the Trauma of Abuse

Parenting has the potential to be one of the most joy-filled and meaningful parts of life, and it can be a source of great inspiration for survivors to keep pressing forward toward a better life, even in the face of challenges. Many survivors who participated in our research told us their children were the reason they decided to leave their abusers, so their children could have safer, happier lives. Often, survivors' desire to be a better parent helps them find courage within themselves they never knew they had. In my own life, I know my deep desire to be a good mom to my children has given me the strength I needed to power through difficult days along my recovery journey.

However, parenting can be one of the most stressful parts of life as well. The stress of parenting can push us to the limits of our coping resources and provide seemingly unlimited tests of our patience. Because parenting is both so meaningful and so stressful, it can be a vulnerable area of life in which unresolved emotions and beliefs from your past can arise. Think back to our earlier discussion about the Trauma Backpack. In many ways, parenting is like running a marathon, although certainly with many "sprints" along the way. Parenting requires patience and endurance to navigate the many changes that happen as children move into different phases of development. Just imagine how much more difficult it is to navigate the stressors and challenges of parenting if you're still carrying a lot of lingering effects of trauma with you. For survivors who had children with and have to have ongoing contact and interaction with their abusers, these ongoing interactions combined with unresolved emotions from the past can create a perfect storm that leads to major difficulty in the area of parenting.

The stress of parenting can be a trigger for a trauma response in survivors. Take time to identify which aspects of parenting stress might be most triggering for you. Here are a few examples to help you consider how this concept of parenting as a trigger might apply to you:

- One survivor has a child who often yells and uses defiant, disrespectful behavior, and this leads her to remember times when her abuser yelled and showed a lack of respect and consideration of her feelings.
- Another survivor becomes distressed when her young children use any form of verbal aggression toward siblings and is afraid her children will become abusive as adults.
- A third survivor feels depressed and anxious when he can't spend holidays with his children, and this reminds him of how his abuser used a long, drawn-out battle in custody court as a way to carry out further abuse and hurt his relationship with his children.

Can you relate to any of the above examples or think of other ways that your own parenting-related experiences trigger hurt and pain for you? Of course, parenting stress on its own can be intense, so it may be difficult to determine the extent to which you're having a normal reaction to the stress of parenting or if you're facing a trigger for a trauma response. Two ways to begin teasing this apart are first, by considering whether your emotional responses to these stressors seem out of proportion to the circumstances, and second, monitoring your thought processes after stressful situations to see if you start thinking back to the past in the middle of these situations.

As wonderful as parenting can be, it also can be stressful, tiring, and unpredictable. The demands of parenting are difficult even in the best of circumstances, and all parents have moments when they feel pushed to the limits of their abilities and patience. Parenting also can bring up feelings of insecurity and inadequacy, and this is especially true if you have a history of being in a relationship with someone whose words and actions led you to feel unworthy or broken. In an earlier chapter, we covered how to regain control of your thoughts, and this is especially important in the area of parenting. Identify negative thinking patterns you develop in the area of parenting (e.g., "I'm not strong enough to handle this," or "Maybe I really am a bad parent like my abuser said I was") and intentionally replace those thoughts with more empowering, positive, and true statements (e.g., "I can handle this," and "I am a loving parent and am doing the best I can today").

Many survivors spend some time as a single parent, especially if they had children with their abusers, and being a single parent is no easy task.

Managing the household on your own, dealing with financial challenges, and balancing work and family life are common challenges for single parents. Life as a single parent can feel draining and isolating at times, so it's especially important for survivors who are single parents to be proactive and intentional about building a supportive social network. This is true even if single parents eventually remarry or find a lasting partnership. Blended families and step-parenting roles are complicated, so all of the different possible family configurations survivors may experience after abuse can benefit from positive support from others.

Two ways survivors can manage parenting challenges in the aftermath of abuse are (1) to be proactive about identifying and managing emotions and (2) building communication and parenting skills.

First, work toward developing mindfulness of your emotional responses to parenting situations. Whether in the moment or after a stressful parenting situation has passed, identify what you were feeling and what specifically about that situation led to you feeling that way. Stressful parenting situations often demand immediate responses, but even taking a quick, two-second pause during the situation can help you gain greater awareness of your emotions in these moments. As you become more adept at noticing your emotions in these stressful circumstances, begin also to be more intentional about choosing how to manage them. Again, focus here on taking steps to manage your immediate emotions in the moment, such as by taking a brief time-out for yourself (and possibly your child) to calm down or practicing a quick self-care or relaxation strategy, like taking deep breaths. Once the immediate situation has passed, consider when and how you can address any larger emotional issues or trauma responses at a later, safe time, such as in your next counseling appointment or through journaling. When you're dealing with intense emotions related to parenting, focus on your and your child's emotional and physical safety in the moment, but also look for ways to build your capacity for managing similar emotions in the future.

Second, build your overall communication and parenting skills. We'll cover specific communication strategies for talking about your experiences with abuse in the next section, but for now, we'll focus on the overall value of developing stronger relationship and parenting skills to help navigate the ups and downs of parenting. This is true for all parents, not just those who've faced abuse. All parents can benefit from intentional efforts to learn about effective relationship skills, such as communication and conflict management, as well as knowledge and skills to enhance their parenting abilities. It's often said that "kids don't come with instruction manuals." While there always will be some element of figuring out parenting as you go along, there also are many great resources for learning basic relationship skills and parenting strategies that can offer valuable support so you don't have to figure out everything on your own!

Effective relationship and parenting skills are especially valuable for survivors because they can help you more effectively communicate your needs and expectations, set and maintain boundaries, and understand unique developmental needs of children at different stages. The first two of these points (i.e., effectively communicating your needs and expectations and setting and maintaining boundaries) are common challenges for survivors. The nature of an abusive relationship is that an abuser often doesn't care about your needs and expectations or about honoring your boundaries. So, parents with a history of abuse may need to pay special attention to developing these skills as a way of fostering healthy relationships with their children. Also, understanding how children's developmental needs change over time is valuable because these needs intersect with how children respond to stress, which is relevant for children who've been directly or indirectly impacted by trauma.

Before we move on to strategies for talking with children about your experiences with abuse, we'll end this section on a more positive note. Of course, parenting can be stressful, especially if it gives rise to painful emotions or reminders of past abuse. However, parenting also is a wonderful area for self-reflection and meaning-making for survivors in the aftermath of abuse. I encourage you to reflect on how your role as a parent has an even deeper sense of meaning and purpose in your life as a result of your past experiences with abuse. What are your hopes and dreams for your children? What do you want for them in terms of their future lives and relationships with others? How might your experiences with the dark side of relationships offer you wisdom and insights to pass along to help them build healthy relationships? And, how can your love for your children help fuel your motivation for continuing your recovery journey as you work toward building a positive, fulfilling life for you and for them?

Talking with Children about Your Experiences with Abuse

There are many ways the topic of abuse might come up with your children. If you're open and speak publicly about your experiences with abuse, they probably already know some of your story. On the other hand, you may never have told your children about your experiences, or you may be wondering about the best time and way to bring this topic up with them. It's also possible the topic comes up, but the children have no idea a question they asked had anything to do with abuse, such as a child who asks, "Why did you and Daddy get divorced?," without knowing the reason was abuse.

Talking with children—and even deciding whether to talk with children in the first place—about your experiences with abuse can be a complicated issue for survivors. With respect to deciding whether to talk with your children about your experiences with abuse in the first place, there are many factors to consider. Most importantly, there are no right or wrong answers here, and you can figure out what makes the most sense and is the best decision for your family. You may have reasons you've already had to talk with your children about the abuse, such as if they witnessed it. Although many parents wish they didn't have to talk about difficult subjects like violence and abuse with young children, the reality for children who've witnessed abuse directly is they've already been exposed to the violence. *Not* talking about abuse with children who have seen it or been directly impacted by it can be more harmful than talking about it, although of course it's important to talk about it with them in developmentally appropriate ways.

Another reason many survivors want to talk with their children about abuse is because they recognize the potential increased risk for experiencing future abuse as a victim or perpetrator for children who have faced or witnessed abuse. Keep this next important point in mind: *Your children are not destined to grow up and become an abuser or a victim just because their lives were impacted by abuse during childhood.* This is true whether you were the first person in your family to experience abuse or if there's a long pattern of violence and abuse that crosses generations in your family. Be empowered to know that with every step you take in your personal healing journey, you're also taking important steps toward helping your children build healthy, nonviolent lives. Try to resist feeling guilt or worry that your experiences with abuse will become a curse for your children, and try to channel those negative feelings into positive motivation to help your children learn to build and maintain healthy relationships throughout their lives.

One of the most important considerations when deciding how to talk with your children about your experiences with abuse is their age and developmental stage. If you aren't familiar with different phases of child development, consider seeking educational resources or a parenting class on this topic. Even with a basic understanding of childhood development phases, remember each child develops in their own unique way. Some children are more mature or immature than other children their age, so consider your child's maturity level to figure out the best approach to these conversations. If you have more than one child, each one may require a different approach.

Find developmentally-appropriate ways to have sensitive conversations with children. For example, with very young children, you may find it helpful to use simple language and age-specific resources to talk about abuse and related topics. For example, one set of resources I love is from Sesame Street in Communities (www.sesamestreetincommunities.org). They've developed wonderful tools that use familiar Sesame Street characters to help parents and professionals talk about sensitive topics with children ages 0–5. In particular, one topic they address is trauma, and these resources may be helpful for children who've been impacted by abuse. For older children or teens, seek out resources that explain abuse and other related topics (e.g., mental health issues, divorce) using appropriate language the child can understand. Also, a professional counselor or therapist can be helpful with having difficult conversations with children of any age.

Talking about experiences of abuse can be especially complicated if your abuser was their other parent. Be mindful of legal or custody rules or guidelines you need to follow when talking about the other parent. Often, parenting guidelines in custody orders state that parents may not speak negatively about the other parent in front of the children. If your children witness their other parent's abusive behavior toward you, you may want to seek legal advice for clarity on what you can and cannot say about their other parent to them, especially if the children ask specific questions about the abuse.

Avoiding Speaking Negatively About the Other Parent

In general, it's wise for parents in separation, divorce, or co-parenting situations to avoid speaking negatively about the other parent. Children can benefit from close, positive relationships with any parent figure in their lives. If your abuser is the other parent of your child or children, keep in mind that it is *possible* they could be a good parent despite the horrible things they've done to you. Of course, just because something is possible, doesn't necessarily mean it will be true! But, it is theoretically possible that someone who is abusive toward a romantic partner could act differently toward their children or other people in their lives. And, even if your abuser is just generally an all-around bad person, keep in mind that if you speak badly of them to your child, you risk looking like you're stooping to their level. With all this in mind, as best you can, try to stay positive in your conversations with your children about their other parent, or at least try to stay neutral instead of making negative comments. For example, you might say, "I want you to have a positive relationship with your (mom/dad)," or "Your (mom/dad) is doing the best they can." As best you can, try to stay positive, find ways to avoid negativity, and use positive language about your children's other parent in ways that don't feel like you're lying or compromising your integrity.

When the Other Parent Hurts You in Front of Your Children

One unique situation that may arise when you share children with your former abuser is that your abuser might display abusive behavior in front of the children, such as if they use mean words or an aggressive tone of voice with you in front of them. This is a highly complex and tricky situation to navigate, especially if you're legally required to not speak negatively about the other parent in front of the children. You may want to seek legal guidance about this topic, especially if there are pending legal or custody issues between you and the other parent. However, one possible way you could respond is being clear about renouncing the behavior, while also carefully avoiding making global, negative statements about the other parent. Look at the difference between the following two possible responses to this situation:

> Global, negative response: "Your dad is such a jerk! I hope you just saw the way he talked to me. He's a horrible person!"

> Behavior-focused response: "I'm upset about the words your dad just used to talk to me. I want you to know that way of talking to me is not okay by him or anyone else."

It would be natural to be upset and emotionally reactive if your abuser just acted aggressively toward you in front of your kids. So, the global, negative response will be tempting, especially if you don't have self-care strategies to regain your composure quickly. However, do your best to stay calm and use the behavior-focused response as a way to avoid speaking negatively about your children's other parent, while also letting them know abusive words and behaviors are not acceptable. If you think this situation is likely to occur between you and your former abuser, it's wise to plan ahead for how you might respond, and consider what impact any possible responses might have on your children. For example, if you choose to walk away or close the door to your house if your abuser does something to hurt you in front of your children, you may want to explain your decision to your child. A valuable lesson you can teach your children is, "You do not need to participate in every fight or argument you're invited to." Again, you'll want to do all you can to address these complicated situations in a way that teaches your children that abusive behaviors aren't okay, but also avoids speaking negatively about your partner.

When Your Children Ask Difficult Questions

Kids have a way of asking questions that seems simple to them, but actually are very complicated to answer. All parents find themselves struggling to know how to answer their children's questions at times, but the complexity of these questions is multiplied when a family has been impacted by something as difficult as abuse. When your children ask big, complicated questions—such as "Why did you get divorced?," or "Why did mommy/daddy hurt you?"—take time to plan your response. If these questions catch you off guard, it's okay to let your child know you'd like to think about the question and talk about it later. However, it's important to respond and answer your children's questions in age-appropriate ways. Some parents get so uncomfortable with certain questions that they just change the subject or avoid answering questions all together. However, if your long-term goal is to have a relationship in which your children feel safe and supported in talking with you about virtually anything, it's important to set the stage early on by showing you're open to having difficult conversations.

One way to handle difficult questions and answers is by starting with the minimum amount of information needed, and then let your child guide the conversation by asking follow-up questions, if they have any. Sometimes, children are satisfied with shorter answers, and other times, they'll have more and more questions. Try to use words that are understandable by children in their developmental stage. Again, you might find it helpful to use books or other resources to help with these conversations. It's also okay to have boundaries and limits on what you will and won't disclose to your children, and this may include the points above about trying to avoid speaking negatively about their other parent. There will be times when you simply can't answer your children's questions, and it's okay to say, "I don't know the answer to that question," or otherwise acknowledge there are some questions you can't answer. You'll have to find the right wording for you and your children, but below are a couple examples of wording that could be useful to consider:

> "When you're an adult, and if you still want to know my answer to these questions, I'll be happy to talk with you then. For now, I just need you to trust that as your parent, I'll always try to make the best decisions I can at any point in time."

> "I don't know why mommy/daddy chose to do that to me. Sometimes people act in certain ways because they're hurting inside or they don't know anything different. What's most important to me now is that you know I'm here for you and want you to be happy and safe."

If the overall tone of your relationship with your children is openness and honesty, then they will likely be more understanding, trusting, and comfortable asking questions even when they stumble into questions you can't answer.

Keeping an Open Door for Ongoing, Honest Conversations with Your Children

Having open, honest communications with your children is an ongoing process, not a one-time conversation. It's likely there will be conversations that happen in your normal, day-to-day life, as well as there will be developmental and life transitions when challenging topics arise, such as when children start dating or leave for college, if there are changes to your custody schedule, and if you get remarried. It's likely your children will need extra help and support at different points in their lives, and new questions will arise as they grow and learn. Be willing to talk with them when they need support, and don't underestimate the value of seeking support from a counselor to help navigate these conversations.

Most parents hope to protect and shield their children from dark, scary things of the world. However, if your children's lives have been impacted by abuse, then it's likely your children already have been exposed to some difficult, sensitive topics. It's important to help your children be kids and give them chances to have fun, play, and laugh. You might try to keep separation between times for difficult conversations and times for fun. You can help model for your children that a well-rounded person is able to both experience joy and navigate serious topics.

Honesty is another important quality to nurture in your relationship with your children, although with appropriate boundaries in terms of not disclosing overly personal or negative information with your children. Avoid lying to your children or pretending things didn't happen that they know did happen. Dishonesty can invalidate your children's perceptions and emotions and make them feel dismissed or like their needs or feelings aren't important. Also, be mindful of not making promises to your children you can't keep. For example, you can't make promises about another person's behavior. If their other parent is an inconsistent parent, avoid promising your children that their other parent will always be there for them. Bring honesty to other topics of conversation as well. As another example, if your financial situation has been negatively impacted by the abuse you experienced, avoid making promises about paying for things you're not sure you'll be able to afford. Parent-child relationships benefit from maintaining a spirit of honesty and openness so children can grow up viewing their parents as a source of support, information, and guidance.

Talking with children about difficult topics is never easy, and it's especially challenging for families impacted by abuse. These conversations can be especially difficult if you're feeling emotionally overwhelmed by other aspects of your recovery process. Reach out for support and guidance from professionals and trusted friends and family members as you navigate these challenging conversations, and keep your love and concern for your children at the front of your mind to guide and motivate you through the challenging moments.

Attempting to Co-parent with Your Former Abuser

When parents separate or divorce, the "gold standard" approach to raising their children is often thought to be co-parenting, in which parents maintain separate households but work collaboratively to make joint decisions, use a similar parenting style to instill shared values, and put the children's needs in front of differences or tension between the parents. Co-parenting is thought to lead to the best outcomes for children because parents prioritize the children's needs and are committed to working through differences. For many survivors, this ideal of co-parenting is difficult, if not impossible, to achieve. Many behaviors and characteristics that are common among abusers come out in parenting-related experiences. If you struggle in your experiences of trying to co-parent with your former abuser, know that you're not alone.

For many survivors, parenting with an abusive partner is nothing short of a nightmare. Parenting can become the new arena in which the abuser tries to exert power and control over their former victim since they no longer have access through the romantic relationship. Sometimes, in a court context, relationships between an abusive partner and survivor are called "high-conflict" custody cases. However, in reality, the "conflict" often is one-way, with the abuser using parenting situations to make life as difficult as possible for the survivor. Often, *parallel parenting* is an alternative to co-parenting in these situations. Parallel parenting refers to two parents who operate as independently as possible and coordinate as minimally as needed. In essence, with parallel parenting, each parent agrees, "You do your thing, and I'll do mine." Parallel parenting can be a useful starting point for parenting in the aftermath of an abusive relationship.

Even parallel parenting can be difficult to achieve with an abusive other parent. First, the "You do your thing, and I'll do mine" assumption of parallel parenting can be heart-wrenching if your former abuser does things as a parent you believe are potentially harmful for your children. This is especially true if you believe the other parent is doing things that put your children at risk *because* they're trying to hurt you. It's difficult to just step aside and watch quietly when that's happening. On the other hand, if you express your concerns to the other parent, it's likely you'll be met with resistance, accusations, or further abuse.

Another reason parallel parenting can be difficult with an abusive other parent is because the abusive parent might try to disallow you to "do your thing" as a parent. It may feel as if they want to do their own thing, but they will continue to berate and harass you and disparage your parenting decisions. You might find yourself fielding frequent criticisms about your parenting abilities, mental health, and your own level of cooperation with them. Even if you've worked hard to attempt to cooperate with them, their manipulative approach to relationships can mean they'll claim you're the uncooperative one.

If you're struggling to co-parent or parallel parent with your former abuser, it's important to be intentional in your approach to interacting with them. You may even want to think of yourself as doing *defensive parenting* or *highly-boundaried parenting*, or whatever term makes sense to you to describe your experiences. You may feel like you're constantly on the defensive against your abuser's power and control tactics in parenting. Either way, having clear, strong boundaries is essential to protect yourself and establish the best possible context for parenting. It's also critical to surround yourself with a supportive parenting team or community, including professionals (such as parenting educators, counselors, and your children's teachers, coaches, and other significant adults in their lives) and informal sources of support (such as trusted friends, neighbors, and extended family members). Be proactive about asking for support from your parenting team, and consider how each person offers a unique positive influence on you and your children Parenting with an abusive other parent is not for the faint of heart, and you can expect there will be many challenges, so building a strong support network is essential so you won't feel alone along the way.

You can also empower yourself as a parent by learning positive parenting skills and knowledge, which is crucial to be able to counter claims by the other parent that you're not doing a good job. It may be helpful to map out possible responses to parenting situations so you'll be prepared when challenges arise. For example, if you have concerns the other parent may be putting your children's safety or wellbeing at risk, you might want to discuss those concerns with your attorney to determine what risks can be addressed legally or by calling your local Child Protective Service agency. As another example, parenting challenges may arise related to scheduling, especially around special days like holidays. To address these challenges, be proactive about discussing these scheduling issues, and maintain easy access to legal documents that spell out schedule requirements so you can refer to those when needed.

In addition, use effective communication strategies for interacting with manipulative, hostile communication from the other parent. One useful resource for learning these communication strategies is the High Conflict Institute (www.highconflictinstitute.com), and especially their resources on BIFF (Brief, Informative, Friendly, and Firm) responses. Although it's unlikely you can fully remove all frustration from your interactions with the abusive other parent, by empowering yourself with knowledge and communication skills, you can become better equipped to manage the challenges they'll put you through so you can stay strong and effective in your parenting.

Navigating Child Custody and Family Court Issues

One expensive, time-consuming arena in which parenting-related abuse tactics can play out is in child custody and family court. Court processes can take years to resolve, so they can be a lasting way for abusers to inflict harm upon their former partners. This section addresses strategies that can be used to navigate these challenges, although it's in no way intended to be a substitute for sound legal advice from a qualified attorney. In fact, one of the most important people to have on your side if you're up against your former abuser in court is a knowledgeable attorney, especially one who is familiar with the dynamics of abusive relationships.

Of course, attorneys can be expensive, so this can be prohibitive for many survivors. If you don't feel you're able to afford an attorney, it's worth the time and effort to seek out free or reduced-cost legal resources in your community. In some communities, there are specialized nonprofit legal resources for survivors of domestic violence. Your local domestic violence agency should be able to provide referrals to any resources of this nature, such as legal clinics offered through law schools in your area or lawyers who offer pro bono services for survivors. If at all possible, try to have the most qualified attorney you can find and afford on your side. One of the common experiences for survivors in family court is that their abusers controlled the finances in the relationship, and therefore they're able to afford an expensive attorney, and the survivor's stark financial situation prohibits them from accessing quality legal advice. There are no easy answers to this situation, but truly the value of a quality attorney in these cases cannot be underemphasized.

Try to find a lawyer who treats you with respect and takes an educational approach to working with clients. You deserve to be represented by a lawyer who doesn't speak down to you, but who does provide you with information you need to make the best decisions about how to proceed through all aspects of the case. It's also helpful to work with a lawyer who is realistic about the possible outcomes of the case. There's no way to guarantee any possible outcomes when it comes to legal proceedings, so be cautious if an attorney promises you'll win your case. In particular, working with a lawyer who understands the tactics abusers use is important because the abuse dynamics can play out throughout the court case. If at all possible, you'll want to have an attorney on your side who'll be able to recognize when court processes are being used as a power and control tactic, who can prepare you for how to respond to questions about abuse if they come up in court, and who can educate the judge about unique safety considerations involved in your situation.

Facing your abuser in court is a scary process, so consider having other people in your support network with you. For example, you may want to work with a victim advocate through a local domestic violence agency or invite some close friends and family members to accompany you to court for encouragement and to help you feel safer in the courtroom. Outside of the courtroom, this is another area in which it can be helpful to be working with a qualified professional counselor who's knowledgeable about abuse and the complexities of child custody and court issues.

One of the most stressful aspects of custody court is the uncertainty it involves, especially as it relates to your children. Even if you think you have a strong case, there's still a chance a judge will rule in favor of your abuser, or even result in a final ruling involving some sort of compromise that you feel is not in your children's best interest. Again, it's helpful to talk through all possible outcomes with your attorney, especially so you can weigh the risks and benefits of trying to mediate or settle the case out of court.

Because of how horrific the experience of family or child custody court can be, even if you "win" your case, you may still feel like you've lost so much in the process, and those losses may include the stress and energy you faced, major financial costs, and a huge amount of time that you had to spend on the case. In many ways, even though usually one side "wins" and the other "loses," when it comes to custody court, there really are no winners. Children especially may lose big in these cases, even if they never know they happened. The damage to the co-parenting relationship from court cases can be irreparable, although sometimes parents are able to still establish an amicable relationship after court processes end.

If you "win" your case, be cautious that the abuser may take their anger at the outcome out on you. If you become concerned your safety is at risk, be sure to talk about your concerns with your lawyer, a victim advocate, the judge, and/or law enforcement so safety protections can be put in place, such as mandating that custody exchanges happen in safe, public locations. On the other hand, if you "lose" your case, in addition to being concerned about the implications of that decision on your children, know the abuser may continue to hold the outcome of the case over your head, such as by saying something like, "The judge agreed with me that you're unstable/not a good parent." Again, consider any needed safety protections, and be open with the involved professionals about possible next steps if things get worse for you or your children after any new custody requirements are put in place.

Regardless of the outcome of a custody case, it's important to recognize that court processes may become another layer of trauma for you, and if so, consider how to heal and recover from those experiences. Seek extra emotional support or counseling to help you heal. It can be helpful to treat the trauma of the court process as a separate traumatic experience that requires separate healing, in addition to the trauma of the original abuse you faced. Your abuser may have paid their lawyer a lot of money to rip you apart in court, and you may need to take time and effort to work through the hurtful words the lawyer said so you can heal from those hurts as well.

Take steps to promote your safety, healing, and wellbeing in areas of life in which you were impacted by your experiences in family court. For example, consider seeking added protections or guidelines to promote your and your children's emotional and physical safety during custody exchanges. You may need to address the financial implications of the court processes as well. Work toward developing a plan for paying off debt or making up for lost income from missing work due to court appearances. Also, be cautious as you look to the future, as it's possible that your abuser will take you back to court again, and possibly again and again and again. This is an unfortunate experience shared by a relatively small proportion of the survivors who participated in our research related to See the Triumph, but it is a possibility, especially if you have a particularly vindictive abuser who has access to many financial resources. Once your journey through family court is over (or possibly as you reach significant milestones along the way if you anticipate a long, drawn out case or series of cases), consider marking the occasion with a ritual or celebration. For example, you might want to plan a special trip, a night out with friends, or even simply taking time to write down your story of the court experience to share with your close friends. The journey through family court can be a long, harrowing one, and even if the process and outcome were difficult, try to focus on the strength and courage you demonstrated along the way.

Conclusion

Parenting is difficult, and especially if you're parenting in the aftermath of abuse. Parenting stress can be overwhelming and may even trigger a trauma response stemming from past abuse. Specific challenges survivors may face include uncertainty about how to talk with their children about their experiences with abuse, extreme difficulty trying to co-parent or parallel parent with a former abuser, and potential ongoing legal and custody battles. Facing these challenges can feel like an impossible task at times, but keep in mind that you are your child's parent for a reason, and you have a unique and important opportunity to be a role model for them and help them grow into kind, loving adults. As much as possible, try to keep this long-range view in mind, and let your hopes and dreams for your children's future motivate you to take on any challenges that arise. Your parenting—as well as how you live your own life—can help your children learn to build safe, healthy relationships, as well as help them to have positive mental and emotional health and overcome any abuse-related challenges they face. Finally, know that you're not alone in facing challenges as a parent whose life has been touched by abuse. Try to connect others who understand the challenges you've faced to help you feel supported along the way.

8

DEALING WITH CONTINUED ABUSE

"I eventually left him and moved in with my sister and her husband. He continued to verbally and emotionally abuse me by using my children when he would come to get them on weekends. After 2 years, he decided he would try and run from paying child support and moved to another state."

~ Domestic Violence Survivor

"The abuse hasn't yet ended—he has been slowly bankrupting me in divorce court for years."

~ Domestic Violence Survivor

"I ended the relationship. There was a long, contentious aftermath lasting longer than the relationship."

~ Domestic Violence Survivor

"I divorced him. However, he continued to stalk me until he died 11 years later."

~ Domestic Violence Survivor

"It took me almost 3 years of not being with him to get him to leave me alone. I literally was stalked at my job and I moved. He went to prison for aggravated assault."

~ Domestic Violence Survivor

One of the biggest misconceptions about abusive relationships is that once an abusive relationship ends, the abuse stops as well. For some survivors, the end of a relationship with an abusive partner *is* the end of the abuse. In our See the Triumph-related research, we've heard from many survivors who told us the abuse stopped because their abuser abandoned them, left them for another partner, died, or was incarcerated, among other reasons why the end of their relationship led to the end of the abuse. However, we also heard from many survivors who faced continued abuse even long after their relationships ended. In fact, even some of the reasons listed above (i.e., abandonment, infidelity, and incarceration) may not lead to the abuse stopping, such as survivors whose abusers continue to harass them from jail.

For many survivors, abuse doesn't stop just because their relationship with their abuser ends. The reality for many survivors is that abuse continues long after their relationship ends, and sometimes indefinitely, although abuse might look different from when the abuser had more direct access through the relationship. As we covered in the last chapter, one major way that abuse can continue is through legal proceedings related to child custody and family court, as well as through other aspects of parenting, such as custody exchanges or sabotaging parenting decisions. Other ongoing legal issues may arise through which abusers can continue to perpetuate harm, such as divorce proceedings, sharing property or businesses, long-lasting criminal court cases, and other situation-specific legal issues. There are other ways abusers may continue to abuse survivors after the relationship ends, such as by smearing their reputations, turning other people against them, and harassing or stalking them physically or electronically. In this chapter, we'll first explore ways abusers can continue to perpetuate abuse even after relationships end, and then we'll cover strategies for promoting your safety and personal wellbeing if your abuser continues to try to hurt you, even long after your relationship ended.

How Abuse Can Continue: When "No Contact" Isn't Possible

Because of the continued harm former abusers can create in survivors' lives, some experts recommend going "no contact" and cutting all ties with abusers. This is a wise idea if at all possible, and if so, it's a good idea to make clear to your abuser you intend to have no further communication or contact with them and they don't have your permission to contact you for any reason other than essential financial or legal matters, and even then it may be helpful to indicate they should only contact you through your attorney. Documenting (e.g., in writing or through a photograph) that you've established this boundary can be an important step in protecting yourself if your abuser attempts future harassment or stalking.

In some cases, however, it's not possible to fully cut all ties with your abuser, especially if you share custody of children, live nearby to each other in a small community, or share social connections. With legal issues like shared custody, you may be legally required to have at least some level of communication and contact with your abuser. You may not have a choice about needing to interact with them. Even if you theoretically have a choice about other reasons, such as where you live and who your friends are, removing yourself from situations in which you may have to interact with your former abuser might also mean removing yourself from a community or friendships you love and that offer support. There are no easy answers here, and it's wise to seek professional support, such as from a counselor, to help make these decisions.

Aside from cases in which you're legally required to have contact with your abuser or you have other strong reasons to potentially cross paths, you may be tempted to leave open a door of communication with your abuser for other reasons. One reason may be you're holding out hope your abuser might one day reach out to you to apologize for their abusive actions, and you may think this could be helpful to your healing process. While it's certainly possible someone who's been abusive in the past can change their ways, extreme caution is warranted here as well. Both my professional and personal experiences have taught me that someone who's abusive only very rarely offers a genuine apology. Often, even when apologies are stated, they're used more as a manipulation tactic rather than as a sincere indication of remorse. Think back to what we discussed earlier in this book about the Cycle of Violence, and especially the honeymoon phase. Within this cycle, abusers often offer insincere apologies as a way to trap partners in the relationship. While we can always hope people who are abusive will change, it's wise to maintain a healthy dose of caution and focus more on deciding how to navigate the decision to forgive your abuser on your own.

As we discussed earlier, the topic of forgiveness can be controversial when applied to abuse. Some people argue that refusing to forgive another person leads only to more hurt and pain for the person who was wronged. These people suggest that unforgiveness can lead to bitterness and resentment that can hinder your ability to trust and develop closeness in other future relationships. However, specific to the context of forgiving someone who abused you, another approach is that it should be up to each person to choose whether or not they want to work toward forgiveness. This follows the empowerment approach underlying most victim services for people who've faced abuse in that each person should be supported and encouraged to make choices that make the most sense for them.

Given the different perspectives on forgiveness, it's important to consider whether the goal of forgiveness resonates with you. If you decide to work toward forgiveness, know that forgiveness doesn't require an apology from the other person, and it can be an internal process you work toward as you process your emotions and experiences related to abuse. My personal viewpoint is that forgiveness can be very helpful for survivors in the recovery process. I view forgiveness as being about processing and releasing negative emotions within yourself that keep you tied to your past, and I think forgiveness doesn't have to mean forgetting the hurt that was done to you. I also believe you can forgive someone but still keep solid boundaries in place, and forgiveness doesn't mean you automatically give the person you've forgiven full access to your heart. What do you think about forgiveness? You may agree with me or not, but either way, it's helpful to reflect on this, as your views toward forgiveness can help offer clues to how to address this issue in your own healing journey.

The issue of forgiveness is relevant to this chapter's topic on dealing with continued abuse after your relationship has ended. When abuse is ongoing, if forgiveness is a process you're working toward, then it may be a repeated process you need to consider any time new abuse occurs. The process of forgiveness can be grueling and painful as you work through hurts of your past. This process can be extra difficult if it's something you have to do over and over again if your abuser continues to hurt you. However, remember that new hurts bring new opportunities for healing and strength to emerge. You may even find it becomes easier to forgive each time, or you develop a process that works for you to acknowledge and work through the hurts each time. Working through new hurts any time your abuser continues to hurt you isn't easy, but acknowledging each new hurt as a separate opportunity for healing can lead to deeper personal growth and self-awareness.

Some survivors who face ongoing abuse after their relationship ends might start to feel pressure from themselves or from others to "just move on" or to "put the past in the past." If you continue to experience new abusive actions, however, the past can be brought into the present moment, even if your abuser is no longer your partner. This is why the issue of dealing with continued abuse is so important to survivors' long-term healing journey. First, it's important to be proactive about protecting your physical and emotional safety in the face of continued abuse so you can continue moving forward toward recovery. And second, it's helpful to acknowledge your need to heal and recover from new incidents of abuse so you can intentionally address the new incidents in your healing process. In the next section, we'll consider strategies to address continued abuse so it won't derail your progress toward recovery and healing.

Strategies for Promoting Your Safety and Wellbeing While Facing Continued Abuse

Just like it was important to take steps to protect yourself and care for your emotional and mental health *during* your abusive relationship, it's critical to prioritize your safety and wellbeing if your abuser continues to try to hurt you *after* the relationship ends. First and foremost, if you believe your physical safety is at risk at any time, reach out for the appropriate help, such as by calling a 24/7 crisis hotline in your area, reaching out to your local domestic violence agency for support, filing a police report, and/or consulting with your attorney. You don't have to be in a current relationship with your abuser to reach out to those resources. Violence, stalking, and abuse may even be a crime based on the nature of the abuse, and this is true regardless of whether you're currently intimately involved with the abuser.

However, your abuser may continue to attempt to hurt you in ways that aren't necessarily illegal but are still abusive and hurtful nonetheless. It's important to understand the terms or requirements of any civil legal guidelines that your abuser must follow, such as in a custody agreement or order or in the terms of a divorce or separation agreement. It's possible you may not be able to file criminal charges for some actions, but you might have some civil legal options available if your abuser violates these terms or requirements. Speak with your attorney if this applies to you to learn about your options and how to document or keep records of abusive incidents.

Understanding community resources and relevant laws and civil guidelines can help you navigate continued abuse after your relationship is over. But, what can you do about abusive behaviors that are hurtful but don't necessarily cross a line into being illegal or in violation of the rules or terms of an agreement or court order? Let's face it, abusers can be very manipulative and cunning in the tactics they use. They can be skillful in carrying out hurtful actions but not crossing a line into doing things that would make sense to call the police or file a complaint in court. In fact, often abusers who continue to abuse after the relationship ends can shift to more subtle or underground tactics. Or, they may use blatant tactics that exploit social systems and institutions (such as by taking you to court for new custody issues), hurt your social support network (such as by spreading rumors about you), or add unnecessary stress and drama to your life (such as by being uncooperative and argumentative about parenting matters).

Every situation is unique, so you'll want to consider many factors to determine the best plan that will work for you for navigating continued abuse. Some factors to consider include the nature of the abuse, any legal requirements to interact with your abuser, custody guidelines if you share children, the potential impacts of the abuse in different areas of your life (e.g., your career, friendships, future romantic relationships, parenting, and your finances), and how much support you have available from friends, family, and professionals. Once you've considered these and other relevant factors, consider action steps you can take to respond to any acts of continued abuse and work toward limiting your abuser's access to you. Four specific strategies are discussed below for promoting your safety and wellbeing in the face of continued abuse: (1) setting boundaries, (2) considering how to interact and communicate with your abuser, (3) prioritizing self-care, and (4) reaching out for support from your social support network and professionals.

Establishing Boundaries

Trying to set boundaries with someone who uses abusive words and actions isn't easy. Most likely, your abuser has already shown you they don't respect or honor your boundaries. Otherwise, they likely wouldn't have mistreated you in the first place. Be prepared that your efforts to establish and maintain boundaries with your abuser after your relationship ends are likely to be resisted or ignored. It may take a long, long time before you start to see meaningful progress, and this slow process can be frustrating. However, just because it isn't easy to do this doesn't mean it won't be worth the effort. Establishing strong boundaries—even if it takes time and effort—can be valuable for limiting your abuser's access to you, keeping a healthy level of emotional and physical distance between you and them, and protecting yourself and, if applicable, your children from added hurt.

Creating self-protective boundaries in your life and relationships is a healthy step. Boundaries are a way to create safety and comfort in relationships. When you're clear about your boundaries, it can create a sense of freedom in knowing you have protections in place to help keep toxic people out of your life and let supportive, caring people in. As a survivor of abuse, you've likely experienced relationship dynamics in which there were minimal to no boundaries, so you may need to develop skills in setting and maintaining boundaries. This is true for any relationship in your life, but it's especially true in the context of navigating boundary violations by your former abuser.

To help build boundary-setting skills, practice these skills in the context of relationships with different people in your life. Consider asking a close friend or family member to support you in these efforts. It may help to role play communicating about a boundary and then how you might react if another person violates your boundary. If you don't have a friend or family member you feel comfortable asking to support you in this way, a counselor or therapist might be another good source of support. Since you can anticipate it will likely be a challenge setting and maintaining boundaries with your abuser, it can be extremely helpful to practice these dynamics in the context of a safer, more comfortable relationship. Practicing boundary-setting in safer relationships can help you build confidence and skills to apply in the unsafe relationship with your abuser.

Consider whether or not to directly communicate a boundary to your abuser. Often, and especially if it could compromise your safety, it's not necessary to inform your abuser about your decisions about boundaries. However, in some cases, it may help to make clear whether or how you plan to respond to certain behaviors. For example, let's say a boundary you want to set is not tolerating your abuser calling your names or using a hostile tone of voice when talking to you. By communicating your expectations with your abuser, you can prepare them for how you plan to respond if they cross the boundary. For example, you might say, "I won't continue speaking with you if you call me a name or speak in an aggressive tone of voice. If you do this, I'll hang up the phone." Depending on your abuser's level of hostility and aggression, you may need to prepare contingency plans, such as what to do if they continue to call and leave hostile voice mails or if they use equally abusive language over email. You should consult your attorney if there are legal considerations for communicating with your abuser that could be impacted by boundaries you're hoping to institute, such as whether you're required to respond to messages pertaining to your children if there are custody considerations.

In addition to considering boundaries with other people, especially your abuser, it also can be useful to set boundaries for yourself and how you want to act in interactions with them. For example, any time I'm dealing with a difficult person, I try to avoid getting sucked down to their level of interaction. Admittedly, I'm not perfect and make mistakes in this area more than I'd like! However, I try to maintain a positive, respectful tone when interacting with others, even if they don't act that way toward me. Of course, we have to have grace with ourselves when we fall short of our personal boundaries and expectations for ourselves. But, we can foster a sense of integrity and build our character by thinking about how we want to act toward others, and then set those expectations as boundaries for ourselves. So, for example, you might decide some personal boundaries you'll strive to uphold, even when talking with your abuser, include not yelling, cursing, or name-calling. These personal boundaries are also self-protective in the sense that, by maintaining them, you'll be able to look back on your interactions with others and not feel shame or sadness that you stooped to a level you're not proud to have reached.

Learning to set and uphold effective boundaries—especially in the aftermath of having had your boundaries trampled throughout an abusive relationship—is no easy process. It's natural to struggle in the process of building boundary-setting skills. However, learning to set and honor boundaries with yourself and others can be an important part of learning to navigate continued efforts by your abuser to cause you harm.

Being Intentional in Your Interactions and Communications

Be proactive and intentional about when, how, and in which forums you interact and communicate with your abuser. Again, it's important to consider requirements for interactions, such as if you're required to provide information or discuss matters related to parenting based on a custody order. Once you understand the minimum requirements you face, it is wise to limit your communications with your abuser to the lowest possible amount of communication and interactions you can have. Before considering any interaction with your abuser, it may be helpful to pause and ask yourself, "Is it absolutely essential that I interact/communicate with them in this way?" If it's not essential, but there are other compelling reasons you're considering, this could be a good thing to discuss with a counselor, attorney, and/or a trusted friend or family member before responding.

As I mentioned in the last chapter, the High Conflict Institute (www.highconflictinstitute.com) in San Diego is a valuable resource for learning strategies for interacting with people who thrive off of conflict and drama, which describes many people who are abusive. In particular, they've got valuable articles on their website about using BIFF responses, which stands for Brief, Informative, Friendly, and Firm (for example, see www.highconflictinstitute.com/biff-responses). BIFF responses offer a practical approach to communicating with highly conflictual people, and the BIFF response approach aims to minimize opportunities for tension while also communicating essential information.

By keeping a framework like BIFF responses in mind, you can have a quick checklist of questions to ask yourself any time you're engaged in any form of communication with your abuser. Sometimes, it takes a few rounds of editing to get the wording aligned with the BIFF approach. You can ask yourself: "Is this brief? Is it sticking to only the information I need to provide? Is my tone friendly? And, am I being firm about boundaries that need to be set in place?" The BIFF framework can be very helpful in many different potentially conflict-ridden communications, even in other settings like workplace relationships. It's wise to take time to edit and rewrite communications, such as emails or text messages, to avoid possible added conflict, drama, and chaos. Given how complex—as well as potentially dangerous—interacting with an abuser can be, a little extra time up front can help save a lot of time and stress later on.

Of course, abusers often try to create as much trouble and hurt as they can, so there's no foolproof guarantee any approach to communication or interactions with your abuser will change their behaviors. Ultimately, your ideal goal may be to *change* their behaviors, but realistically, it may be better to aim for *influencing* their behaviors by managing your own responses and interactions with them. Think about this as limiting their access to you as best you can. There may be some types of access you simply can't avoid, such as having to see them at custody exchanges, legal proceedings, or at your child's sporting event. However, you can consider different types of access to you, including *physical access* in terms of how close they can get to you, *emotional access* in terms of how much you allow them to see your emotional responses to their words and actions, and *personal information access*, with respect to how much information you share with them about your personal life, such as who you're dating, how you spend your time, and who your friends are. If your abuser pushes your limits in terms of how much access they have to you in these areas, it may be helpful to reflect on how much access you want them to have, and what steps you may need to take to limit their access to you.

Potential in-person interactions warrant special consideration. As always, it's important to manage these interactions in a way that feels safe and comfortable to you. Remind yourself you do not owe anyone any particular way of interacting with them. If you've been raised to be polite and kind, it may seem cold and unnatural to have more neutral or avoidant interactions with your abuser, even with seemingly simple things like not saying "hello" if you see them in public or at an event for your children. Again, even these sorts of simple interactions can grant your abuser access to you, so limiting them may be an important step for you. You may want to explain your decisions about how to interact with your abuser to significant people in your life, such as your children or close friends or family members, but also keep in mind you don't owe anyone and everyone an explanation for decisions you make to promote your physical and emotional safety.

Finally, another type of interaction that can cause distress is if your abuser says lies to you or about you, either through in-person or written communications or by spreading rumors about you to others. As always, it's helpful to think carefully about how to respond and address these issues in as brief, factual, and non-reactive manner as possible. However, providing a written, factual response to untrue statements may be helpful for documenting communications with your abuser if any future legal proceedings arise, and this is another area in which it's wise to seek your attorney's guidance.

Abusers can be very manipulative, deceptive, and relentless in their efforts to engage you in communications and interactions that give them further access to hurt you after your relationship has ended. If they continue to do this, it's not your fault, just like no abuse is your fault. Abuse is always the responsibility of the person who is perpetrating it. Nonetheless, having a solid game plan for how you'll respond to your abuser's attempts to engage you in these interactions can be an important part of establishing boundaries to promote your safety.

Practicing Self-care and Emotional Management

Practicing self-care in the face of continued abuse after the relationship has ended is crucial. Experiencing even more abuse, in addition to the past abuse you're working so hard to recover from already, can be exhausting. It's a lot to process past abuse while also dealing with new abuse, on top of other challenges you're facing, such as work or parenting stress. You may face days when the current abuse, on top of the effects of the past abuse, feel so overwhelming you're not sure how you will make it through. However, it's important to remind yourself to take one day at a time and work through one concern or challenge at a time. Try to break down your recovery process—including recovering from new incidents of ongoing abuse—into smaller steps and work through one concern or challenge at a time.

We've covered a lot of strategies for practicing self-care, coping, and managing your emotions throughout this book, so it's a good idea to review those earlier chapters and apply the skills and resources you identified earlier to help navigate new abusive experiences. Most importantly, be intentional and proactive in using those strategies to prioritize your physical, emotional, and spiritual wellbeing. You'll be in the best possible position to navigate new experiences of abuse when you're as healthy and balanced as you can be, and, of course, be patient and gentle with yourself when you feel overwhelmed or get sucked into drama and chaos. Remember: abuse is never your fault, and even the best attempts to counter continued abuse can fall short. Take care of yourself as you face these continued challenges.

Seeking Support

We've also talked a lot throughout this book about the importance of seeking the right kind of social support, so we won't cover this topic in-depth again here. However, it's important to reiterate the importance of leaning into your support network, as well as professional resources in your community, as you deal with continued abuse. Some people mistakenly believe that resources related to domestic violence only apply when you're currently in a relationship with the abuser, but most domestic violence organizations and service professionals understand abuse can continue long after the intimate relationship ends. Whenever you need help, seek out professional support to help determine what options are available to you, develop a safety plan, and plan ways you can respond to any ongoing abuse you face. If continued abuse warrants it and your safety is at risk, seek legal guidance, call a local crisis or emergency line, and/or reach out to law enforcement to promote your safety. You don't need to be in a current romantic relationship for behaviors to be considered abusive. Most importantly, surround yourself with supportive people (including friends, family members, coworkers, and professional helpers) who understand that your challenges with your abuser continue, even after the relationship has ended.

Conclusion

Abuse can continue long after an abusive relationship ends. You may find yourself wondering, "Will this *ever* end?" In reality, there's no way to predict how long continued abuse may last, and this is very situation-specific to the unique context in your life. We've probably all seen movies depicting domestic violence where an estranged abuser will stop at no cost to track down and hurt their former partner. This is certainly possible, and if your abuser shows signs of being that persistent and obsessed with you, it's important to activate your social network and as many professional helping resources as possible to address all the safety concerns that come along with this level of dangerous abuser.

On the other hand, we've heard from survivors in our research that often, there were reasons many abusers eventually stop trying to hurt their former partners. Sometimes, the abuser gets involved in another relationship and loses interest in trying to engage with their former partner while they focus on their new relationship. In other cases, a former abuser goes to jail or has a permanent protective or restraining order in place that prohibits further contact. For other survivors who share custody with their abusers, the abuse may eventually stop once mandated parenting-related interactions end after the children have grown up. One or both people may move far away and lose contact and avoid the risk of running into each other around town. There are many reasons why abuse may eventually stop, and every survivor's experiences are unique.

I wish I could tell you that if you took certain steps, you could guarantee your abuser will stop trying to hurt you. Unfortunately, there are no guarantees like that, and many abusers persist for a long time in trying to continue to hurt you. Even still, you can work toward putting in place protections and strategies to limit your abuser's access to you and opportunities to cause you harm. If you ever took an introductory psychology class in high school or college, you probably learned about the notion of *reinforcing behaviors*. Basically, this means people are more likely to keep doing behaviors that are reinforced by positive outcomes. Ideally, as you begin putting in place more protections and work on managing your responses to your abuser's attempts to hurt you, they'll see their abusive behaviors are no longer reinforced.

Hopefully, in time, your abuser will learn they can't shake you, and they may begin to back down and leave you alone. Whether or not that happens, however, you can continue to work on your own responses so you can navigate these interactions with your abuser with as minimal hurt as possible. You may even reach a point where you learn to process your emotional responses to new incidents relatively quickly and then keep moving forward in your healing journey. We would never want these new abusive incidents to keep happening—but if they aren't avoidable, then one positive byproduct of working through them is that you'll be able to continue to build your personal strength and see your growth over time. For any new experiences of continued abuse you encounter after your relationship has ended, be intentional about guarding your safety, honoring your emotions, and using practical strategies to continue moving forward in your process of healing and recovering from past, and continued, abuse.

9

BUILDING A STRONG FOUNDATION FOR YOUR FINANCES AND CAREER

> "I went from a pregnant teenage wife that dropped out of high school and became a victim of domestic violence to an independent woman with a college degree with 3 beautiful children. There is nothing weak, dumb, or incapable about myself."
>
> ~ Domestic Violence Survivor

Although intimate partner violence occurs in the context of a romantic relationship, it often has significant impacts on victims' and survivors' careers (including their educational attainment) and finances. In this chapter, we'll look at how to clean up messes from the past in these areas, get clear about where things stand for you now, and, perhaps most importantly, start dreaming and planning for your future.

One way abusers can impact survivors' financial and career wellbeing is through financial abuse, which we'll explore in the next section. However, in addition to the direct effects of financial abuse, there are many other ways your finances and work life may have been impacted by abuse. These include lost jobs due to missing work, financial costs associated with legal proceedings, and diminished confidence to pursue your goals because of being worn down physically and emotionally by your abuser.

On top of all the other emotional, health-related, and social consequences of abuse, it would be natural to feel overwhelmed if your finances and career aren't where you want them to be right now. Also, you may feel like your financial or work situation makes it more difficult for you to address your healing in other areas of your life, such as if you don't have money to get things you need for your children or find a safe, affordable place to live. It can take time to move yourself from where you are now to where you want to be financially and in your career, but it *is* possible to build a solid financial foundation and work toward a meaningful, rewarding career.

As hard as rebuilding your life may be, keep in mind this is your opportunity to make decisions for yourself, and you can do this with the freedom you have currently from your abuser. Taking positive steps forward toward a new vision for your future is exciting, but also scary. But, if you know anything as a survivor of abuse, it's knowing how to look scary situations in the face and find your way through them. Even if you still haven't fully embraced your identity as a strong, empowered person, know you possess loads of personal strength within you. You survived a horrible abusive relationship, after all. Working toward financial and career goals is likely to bring challenges your way, and you can work through and overcome these, just like you're overcoming the other impacts of the abuse.

Your experiences with abuse may have forced you into financial and career situations you wouldn't want to be in, but do your best to keep a positive perspective and embrace this opportunity to rewrite your life course. Cleaning up past messes and working toward future goals can be difficult. As you face challenges along the way, remind yourself this is an important part of your story of triumphing over abuse. Let's get started by exploring ways to work through negative lingering effects of abuse on your finances and career.

Cleaning Up Past Financial and Career Messes

If you feel like your finances or career are a complete mess after your experiences with abuse, you are not alone. Check out these quotes from survivors who shared their stories with us in our See the Triumph-related research:

Financial Impacts of Abuse

"It took me years to get back on my feet, and I still have not recovered financially from the secondary trauma created as a result of the assault."

"This financial stress is a major PTSD trigger for me."

"After leaving him, I did have to declare bankruptcy to survive on the little money I had left."

"It has taken years and years to pay off debts that I incurred while with my abuser."

"The costs of treatment, medication, and emotional toll have been immeasurable."

"I went to school and racked up $48,000 in student loans, other bills, especially medical bills."

"He withheld items of mine adding to my expenses to have a household and living items: Car, clothes, furniture."

"I have spent more than a decent down payment on a house for all the mental and physical effects he had on me."

"My ex refused to pay child support for our children we shared, and to this day he's at least $49,000 in arrears!"

"Once I found the domestic violence center, they provided services at no cost. I still had to pay for treatment for my children."

"To be able to see a therapist has been a privilege, but a financial burden, as the claims are denied by insurance."

"The abuse has had a very bad detrimental impact on my funds. The cost for legal representation alone is staggering. Add the medical and therapy bills the cost goes up into the hundred thousands."

"I am not able to pay the majority of my medical bills that have built up, and my credit rating is very low now."

Career Impacts of Abuse

"Anxiety makes it difficult to concentrate on my job."

"After the assault, the trauma and secondary trauma resulted in loss of my job that I had for 13 years."

"I am still paying off court costs, and am unsure how I will survive next year without a regular full-time job, but my health (physical and mental) is suffering because of the demands of regular work."

"My job and ability to do full time hours have been compromised. I have anxiety and panic attacks and flashbacks."

"I almost lost my job because of him. I missed work because of stress-related illnesses and numerous court appearances during work hours, not to mention the financial consequences."

"The lack of confidence and trust in my abilities has impacted how I feel in terms of security with new jobs and opportunities."

"It was very difficult keeping a job. I wasn't secure in ability to perform job duties, and loud noises would trigger my anxiety."

"I am exhausted, I lack confidence, and I don't trust my abilities."

"I have tried going through workforce development and vocational rehab, but because I already have 2 master's degrees I am 'over-qualified,' and meeting the demands of work or cash assistance programs only adds to control-induced stress."

"I am currently unemployed and living in a motel. I can't find a job with sufficient income to make change, and I need to get some kind of training or schooling so I can make a decent income, but I can't afford school or qualify for student loans."

These statements illustrate the huge financial and career implications of an abusive relationship. Costs can skyrocket quickly, leaving survivors grappling with financial challenges while they're facing the difficult process of healing emotionally and physically. With limited economic resources in hand, many survivors face an arduous journey toward recovery. But just as you're not alone if you've faced negative financial or career impacts of abuse, you also can draw inspiration from other survivors who've taken on the long but rewarding path of financially recovering from past abuse.

Let's take a closer look at how one specific dimension of abuse—financial abuse—can play out in abusive relationships. Financial abuse involves the power and control dynamics that are typical in abusive relationships playing out in financial aspects of a couple's relationship. Financial abuse can take many different forms, including exploitation, fraud, stealing, identity theft, forcing victims to hand over money from their own paychecks, and giving victims an "allowance" in a demeaning or patronizing way (i.e., the allowance is not a mutual decision included in a shared financial spending plan). In safe, healthy relationships, both partners share in financial decision-making and work together toward mutual financial goals. However, in a financially abusive relationship, the abusive partner uses financial resources as a way to exert power and control over the other person.

Related to financial abuse, abusers also may perpetrate educational and/ or employment abuse. Examples of educational abuse include forcing you to miss classes, harassing or stalking you in your school setting, forcing you to help them cheat or otherwise compromising your academic integrity, and forcing you to give them money you set aside for tuition and other educational expenses. Examples of employment abuse including showing up unwelcomed at your workplace, harassing you and/or your coworkers, forcing you to miss work, bad-mouthing you to your employer or coworkers, stalking you at work, and hurting or controlling you in a way that negatively impacts your work performance.

Like other forms of abuse, financial abuse can continue long after an abusive relationship ends. Your former abuser can continue to hurt you financially by filing frivolous lawsuits that keep you spending money on legal representation, failing to pay alimony or child support, stealing your identity, and continuing to attempt to sabotage your work or educational goals. In light of the many ways abusers can hurt their partners financially, educationally, and in their careers, it's no surprise many survivors find themselves dealing with a huge mess once the abusive relationship has ended.

Financial messes can feel debilitating, especially if survivors were left with limited or no financial resources when the relationship ends. Many survivors in our research shared stories about how they were left with no financial resources, and their abusers who had controlled the finances walked away with access to much more money. This often played out in legal situations where the abuser had money to pay for an expensive attorney, and the survivor had virtually no financial resources to afford legal representation. This can become a really harmful cycle, especially if court proceedings lead to reduced financial resources, such as less child support, unequal division of assets in separation or divorce proceedings, or survivors being forced to take on added debt.

With all these potential financial and career ramifications of abuse in mind, you may find yourself dealing with any number of "messes" in these areas of your life, even if it's been a long time since you became free of your abusive relationship. Wherever you're starting from today, know you can clean up these messes and begin working toward a positive, meaningful, and financially secure future. If you feel like your finances or career have become a mess, you may feel sad when you think about time, money, opportunities, or energy you've lost as a result of your experiences with abuse. As we've discussed throughout this book, honor those feelings and acknowledge any disappointments you have.

It's natural to feel angry, frustrated, and discouraged as you work toward overcoming financial and career impacts of abuse. Find healthy ways to process those feelings, such as writing in a journal or processing them with a close friend or counselor. Having a strong support network can be especially valuable in staying on track toward cleaning up financial or career messes, especially if you surround yourself with people who encourage you when you're down. In addition to having a strong support network, explore other strategies to stay motivated. For example, you might try following inspirational people on social media or coming up with a motto or mantra you can say to yourself as a reminder when life throws challenges your way, such as the one of the following: "This is my time," "I can do this," "I'm reclaiming my present and future, regardless of what happened to me in the past," "I have something important to contribute to the world," or "I'm worthy of success and financial security."

Generally speaking, the best way to clean up any mess is by breaking it into smaller steps and taking on a bit at a time. I remember when my children were younger and would make huge messes with toys all over the room. I'd get so overwhelmed by looking at the size of the messes they made, but the best way to clean up these huge messes was simply to start cleaning. Often, I found once I started cleaning, the messes almost always looked worse than they really were. I know there's a big difference between cleaning up a messy room and cleaning up the financial and career ramifications of an abusive relationship. But, almost any big mess or problem is easier to clean when it's broken into smaller steps and then handled one small step at a time. One of the first steps toward recovering financially and in your career is taking an honest assessment of where things stand currently, and we'll look at that step in the next section.

Assessing Your Current Financial and Career Wellbeing

An important step toward reclaiming your future is taking an honest look at what's happening in the present moment. This process can be difficult and even painful. In fact, it may feel easier to stay in a state of denial, such as by not opening bills or by glossing over the process of assessing where you are currently in your educational or career path. Be gentle with yourself and apply coping resources any time you experience discomfort while doing this self-assessment. Understanding where you are now helps you know what steps you'll need to take to build your future. Also, prepare to spend time on this self-assessment process, as you may need to take time to track down information or documents.

Below you'll find sets of questions to help you explore and understand your current financial and career (including educational) wellbeing.

Questions to Understand Your Current Financial Status

- What is your income, monthly and annually?
  ◊ What income do you receive from your job(s)?
  ◊ What income do you receive from child support and/or alimony?
  ◊ What income do you receive from any other sources, such as government assistance or support from family?
- What are your monthly expenses? Consider developing a starter budget you can develop more fully later on. Write the exact or estimated amount you spend on each of the following categories, as well as any other categories that apply to your situation. Write "zero" for any categories that don't apply to you.
  ◊ Housing (e.g., rent or mortgage)
  ◊ Utilities (i.e., electric, water, sewage, natural gas)
  ◊ Transportation (e.g., car payment, gas, repairs)
  ◊ Food, including groceries and eating out
  ◊ Healthcare, including health insurance, prescriptions, appointment fees
  ◊ Savings and investments
  ◊ Entertainment and leisure
  ◊ Debts, not including your car payment or mortgage that were listed above
  ◊ Other categories that apply to you
- What assets do you own?
  ◊ How much equity do you have in your home, if you own or have a mortgage on your home?
  ◊ What is the value of your car, compared to any amount you owe on it?
  ◊ How much money do you have saved in retirement accounts?
  ◊ How much money do you have in investment accounts, outside of retirement funds?
  ◊ How much money do you have available in your checking and saving accounts or in cash?
  ◊ What other assets do you have, such as valuable items or jewelry?
- What liabilities or debts do you owe?
  ◊ What is the balance on your mortgage, if you have one?
  ◊ How much do you owe in student loans?
  ◊ What is the balance on your car loan or lease, if you have one?
  ◊ How much money do you own in personal loans, such as to friends or family members?

◊   How much medical debt do you have?

◊   How much credit card debt do you have?

◊   What, if any, other debts do you owe?

- What other financial concerns are relevant to you right now? This might include upcoming legal expenses, any already-established financial goals you're working toward, or any unique or inconsistent factors impacting the information you gathered above, such as inconsistent child support or a fluctuating income.

- How much financial stress do you feel on a daily, weekly, and monthly basis? What are your biggest stressors, and how well do you manage this stress?

Questions to Understand Your Current Career and Educational Status

- What is your current job? If you have more than one job or any other work you do besides a main job that generates income, include that here.

- What is your current highest level of education you've achieved? Do you have plans or a goal of completing more education in the future?

    ◊   If you started a degree, but didn't complete it, how many credits did you complete? How many credits would you need to finish your degree? If you don't know the answer to these questions, consider reaching out to the school's Registrar and/or Admissions office to gather this information.

- What do you like most about your current job?

- What do you like least about your current job?

- How meaningful or fulfilling is your current job?

- How well does your current job provide financially?

- How much opportunity for advancement, promotions, and/or income growth is there within your current job?

Reflecting on Where You are Now with Respect to Finances, Work, and Education

As you answered the questions above, what, if anything surprised you? Sometimes, doing a financial self-assessment leaves people feeling overwhelmed and disappointed, and for others, it can help you realize you're doing better than you thought you were doing. If you're already pretty organized with your finances and career, you may have easily known the answers to the questions on the list, although bringing everything together in one place might have helped you identify some patterns or gaps in how you manage your work and money.

If you had a difficult time doing this self-assessment on your own, consider seeking help from a qualified, knowledgeable, and respectful professional, such as a financial advisor or career counselor. Seek out professionals who will teach you new information in a respectful way when you don't understand things, as well as who empower you to make decisions for yourself and won't pressure you into making decisions.

Once you've considered the current state of your finances, education, and career, take a step back and reflect on how you feel about where things stand currently. Then, consider how you'd like to feel in the future, and use that future hope to start identifying goals and dreams for your future, which we'll cover in depth in the next section.

Dreaming and Planning for Your Future Financial and Career Goals

Once you've done a full-circle self-assessment of your current financial and career status, it's time to start dreaming about where you want to go in the future. Think about all the information you gathered during the self-assessment, and consider the following question: On a scale from 0 (not at all) to 10 (completely), how much does your current career and financial status match up to what you'd like your finances and career path to look like in the future? Perhaps you're close to your ideal vision for your money and work life, or perhaps you're nowhere near where you'd like to be. It's also possible you don't even know what you want in these areas for your future, and if that's the case, know that being unclear about this is understandable in the aftermath of an abusive relationship in which dreaming of a better future may not have been possible. Through dreaming and planning for your future financial wellbeing and career path, you'll have plenty of opportunities to develop and refine your plans, so don't despair if you're not sure what you want to accomplish in the future right now.

Although you just took time to gain a clear idea of where you are now financially and in your career, I want you momentarily set that current status aside for a little while. This isn't about detaching from reality. Instead, I want you to give yourself freedom to dream without feeling limited by your current circumstances. Below are some questions to help you start dreaming and self-reflecting on where you'd ideally like to see your life go in the areas of finances, education, and career:

- What would you like your career or educational achievements to look like 5, 10, and 20 years from now?
- What financial goals would you like to accomplish by 5, 10, and 20 years from now?
- When you reach your older years, what would you like to be able to look back and say you're most proud you accomplished financially and through your work?
- What kind of financial legacy do you want to leave for your children (or for younger generations in your family if you don't have children)?
- If, at the end of your career, you could win an award for something you did through work, what award would you most want to receive?
- What values are most important to you for your career? Examples of values include making a difference for others, being financially successful, and being a strong leader.

As you start dreaming and planning for your career and financial wellbeing, you may notice past things your abuser said to hurt you might come to your memory. For example, they may have said things to you like, "You're horrible with money," "Nobody would ever hire you," or "You're too stupid to do well in school." You might also face other self-doubts you can't directly trace back to your abuser, but that still make you feel like you need to dream smaller or you don't have what it takes to reach your goals. As best you can, observe those thoughts and feelings, acknowledge them, and try to set them aside. Recognize any abusive lies lingering in your mind, and work on counteracting them with more positive, truth-based beliefs that will help you move toward your goals.

Let's consider an example of how lingering doubts from past abuse can impact survivors' confidence in moving toward a brighter future. Imagine a survivor whose dream is to own her own business and be able to retire when she's 65 with enough money saved up to spend time traveling with friends and family. She's got a clear vision for her future, but she also notices that self-doubts arise along with her dreams. For example, she tells herself, "How can I ever think about owning my own business when I'm $100,000 in debt right now and don't even have a college degree?" Without recapping all the information we covered in Chapter 5 about how to change limiting thought processes, it's important to restate here the need to be proactive about noticing negative beliefs and actively working to replace them with more helpful attitudes that will help you stay motivated and empowered to reach your goals.

One of the best things you can do to overcome doubt, while also aiming for positive dreams and goals, is to take your time and focus on taking small steps forward toward your goals. Even if a dream feels unachievable when you first think about it, try and explore your goal as fully as you can and see what would be involved in making it happen. With the example above, a dream of owning her own business and building a comfortable retirement nest egg might feel overwhelming and unattainable to reach all at once, but starting by taking a business class at the local community college and beginning to save just $5 a week might be a manageable starting point that sets this survivor on the long-term path to achieving her big picture goals.

I encourage you to really dream big for your life. But also, know that dreaming big means different things to different people. Even more important than dreaming big is dreaming about things that are meaningful and important to *you*. Each of us has to build and work toward our own dreams that align with our values and our life circumstances. There's a fine balance here between having big dreams and also staying connected to reality. Of course, we all would probably love the fantasy of winning $200 million in the lottery so we could buy our own private island and hang out on the beach all day! It's okay to fantasize about something like that, but try to dream in a way that's connected to, but not limited by, your current circumstances. In other words, be realistic, but also keep an open mind that even doors that may not seem possible to open right now might be possible for you in the future with the right opportunities and hard work.

Take the time you need to gather information, explore different paths and future directions, connect with others who can offer support and practical advice, and start taking steps toward making your dreams and goals a reality. Start with your hopes and dreams, and then start fleshing those out and mapping out a plan to turn them into achievable goals. Some steps you could take as you enter this next phase of your career and financial wellbeing include the following:

Meet with a Professional Advisor

Depending on your financial, educational, and/or career goals—and even how much clarity you have about those goals—you may benefit from seeking out professional advisors who can help you explore your options and gather information. If you're exploring career options, meeting with a career counselor or coach in your area may be helpful. Some local colleges and universities (including community colleges) allow the public to access certain services within their career counseling centers, or you may be able to connect with career counseling services through a school you attended. Public libraries also can be another source for career information. If you're considering returning to school to start or finish a degree, consider reaching out to that school's admissions office, as well as potentially contacting directly the specific department that houses the program in which you want to study. Financial aid offices also can provide valuable information about funding sources to support your education, including scholarship opportunities. When working toward financial goals, you may find it helpful to meet with a trusted financial planner or advisor. One nonprofit resource for credit counseling is the National Foundation for Credit Counseling (NFCC; www.nfcc.org), which can help connect you with local organizations in your community that offer those services as well. For any professional from whom you seek support, be sure to work with someone who is credible, treats you with respect, and shares guidance but offers you freedom to make the best decisions for yourself.

Do Informational Interviews with People Who've Reached the Goals You Want to Reach

In addition to reaching out to professionals who offer guidance and advice for a living, also consider seeking opportunities to learn from people who are living out the dreams you want to achieve. If you're a single mom who aims to return to college to go to graduate school, ask the program you're considering if they could connect you with a current student or recent graduate who's in the same position. If you're hoping to enter a new career field, try to meet with someone who's been working in that field for several years so you can pick their brain and gather information about that field. If you've got a big financial goal you're working toward, find someone who recently achieved that goal so you can ask them how they did it.

Informational interviews can be a valuable learning tool to help clarify your goals and determine what action steps you can take to make progress toward those goals. Of course, some people won't be open to meeting with you in this way, but most likely, you'll find many people who are happy to offer time to someone who's working toward big goals in life. If you don't know where to start in terms of identifying prospects for these interviews, try starting first with friends and family members, as well as others you know through your current job, neighborhood, or religious/spiritual community, and see if you could find a friend-of-a-friend to start with. Searching for professionals' work bios or organizational websites can be another source of ideas of people to interview.

Keep in mind that the people you may want to speak with are likely pretty busy and goal-oriented, so a brief, polite email introduction and request for a short amount of their time (e.g., 30 minutes) for a phone call or cup of coffee can be a good starting point for these meetings. It's also smart to have a list of questions written out to offer more structure to the interview and maximize your time with them. Some helpful questions to ask include the following: (1) What initially motivated you to want to (get this degree/do this kind of work/reach this financial goal)?; (2) What are the best and hardest parts of your (educational journey/job/financial goals)?; (3) What advice would you offer to someone looking to start on this journey?; and (4) What's one thing you wish you had known when you started your journey that you know now?

Connect with Organizations in Your Community that Offer Supportive Resources

You may be able to connect with organizations in your area that offer tangible support to help you move toward your financial and career goals. This might include educational workshops, mentoring programs, career clothing closets, and financial management classes. Depending on your income, you may qualify for programs that help you find child care, access transportation, or learn about funding sources to start a new business. If you're not sure what types of resources are available, see if there are hotlines you can call to help you navigate and connect with support in your area. For example, many United Ways support a 2-1-1 resource and referral line. Also, don't be afraid to reach out to a friend or professional who you know to be well-connected and ask for their help. Often, people will be happy to help you connect with the right resources in your community even if they can't personally provide the support you need themselves.

Rally Your Support Network

In addition to seeking support from professionals and organizations in your community, lean into your social support system along the way as you work toward your financial and career goals. If you've got friends or family members with special skills or talents, see if they can help teach you what they know. For example, if you have a friend who's good at managing finances, consider asking them to help you develop a monthly budget. Other people in your support network may be excited about the chance to support your progress toward your goals by offering tangible support, such as an extended family member who's willing to watch your children while you attend college classes in the evenings. Beyond these forms of practical support, let your loved ones provide you with emotional support and encouragement as you work toward your goals. Tell your loved ones about your goals, and ask them to check in with you about your progress and help cheer you on along the way. Keep in mind: everyone in your life may not fully support or understand your goals. Try to focus your energy on the people and relationships that offer you support, and you can strengthen your relationships with them by offering them encouragement toward their goals as well.

Seek Out Credible Information

When it comes to pursuing financial, educational, or career goals, knowledge truly is power. The more you know about what it takes to succeed in these areas, the better you'll be positioning yourself for success. A word of caution is necessary, however: there are probably just as many, if not more, sources of *bad* information in these areas as there are sources of good, credible information. Don't believe everything you read, and be mindful about avoiding scams and people who prey on those who are in vulnerable situations. Check out any possible sources of information by searching for reviews online and evaluating if a person or organization is working to truly help you, or if they just want to take your money. Fortunately, there are many valuable, credible sources of support that you can trust. A librarian at your local public library is a great resource for identifying helpful resources and evaluating the credibility of them. It's wise to consult many different credible sources of information and think critically about the information they provide and whether and how to apply it to your life.

Map Out Action Steps to Turn Your Dreams into Plans

Once you've gathered the information you need to help you become clearer about the dreams you want to pursue, you're ready to start turning those dreams into plans! Map out action steps that you can take to move from where you are today to where you want to be. You may have heard the acronym, SMART, to refer to how to set effective goals: Specific, Measurable, Action-oriented, Realistic, and Time-bound. When your goals reflect these characteristics, they're more likely to be met because you can hold yourself accountable to them most effectively.

Any time you feel overwhelmed, consider breaking down bigger goals into smaller, achievable action steps. Remember the abuse recovery process—including financial and career recovery—is a marathon, not a sprint. Be sure to celebrate small successes along the way, and surround yourself with cheerleaders who'll help encourage and support you. In particular, you may want to ask one or more loved ones to become your accountability partners to offer tangible, consistent support and accountability for taking the steps you want to take toward achieving your goals. Having an accountability partner can be especially helpful in talking through difficult decisions and helping you to feel less alone on your recovery journey.

Don't Worry about Being "Late" to Getting Started

Before I started working in my current job as the director of a university-based research center, I worked for 14 years as a professor in a graduate counseling program. During that time, I was often asked by people I knew about my thoughts on whether they should pursue their dreams and go back to school, whether that was finishing an undergraduate degree or starting a graduate program. My answer to that question was always the same: The time will pass anyway. Two years from now (or four years, or however many years it takes!), the time will have passed one way or another, whether or not they did the degree. The question was, how important was it they used that time to get the degree? Education is such a valuable tool for opening new doors to opportunity. Often, people who are afraid of the time commitment involved realize that committing the time to furthering their education will be well worth it. On the other hand, sometimes people realize they don't need formal education or any more degrees to move forward in their careers. Again, mentors and informational interviews can help you determine if that path would be right and helpful for you.

It's never too late to begin pursuing a new goal. I've had the benefit of seeing years' worth of evidence that people of all ages can return to school or start a new career path and find fulfillment and success, even later in life. As a professor, I had students of all ages, including traditional-age college students, as well as those in their 30s, 40s, 50s, 60s, and even a couple in their 70s! Don't let fears that you'll be the only person in your age group or the oldest person in the room stop you from pursuing your goals. With respect to education, many universities even offer specialized offices, such as an "Office for Adult

Students" or an "Office for Nontraditional Students," to offer practical and emotional support for students who return to school later in life.

You might feel out of place or awkward as you take steps toward your goals, especially if you feel like you're late to the game. Remember: You're on your own unique journey, and it's okay if your journey doesn't look like everyone else's. As painful as some aspects of post-abuse life can be, try to see this phase of your life as an opportunity that not everyone has. The truth is, there are a lot of people *your* age, right now, who feel stuck in their current jobs, relationships, or lifestyles, but don't have any impetus to change things, so they stay stuck in unhappy places. You may not have chosen for your life to be disrupted by abuse, but just because you didn't choose it, doesn't mean you can't embrace the opportunity to make the most of this next phase of your life. In fact, one day, you may even find someone reaching out to you to ask you for an informational interview to learn how you achieved your success, and I hope you won't turn that interview down!

Conclusion

Rebuilding your finances or career in the aftermath is no easy task. It's quite possible the abuse left you with a huge mess to clean up, especially if you faced financial, educational, or employment abuse. Even if your abuser didn't hurt you directly in these areas, it's likely your financial and/or career wellbeing was impacted in some ways by the abuse you experienced. These aspects of the recovery process can be very challenging. However, to some extent, these are some of the most practical, tangible aspects of the recovery process. For example, you can actually track your financial progress by looking at numbers—such as, how much money is in your bank account or how much debt you've paid off. Other aspects of the recovery process are much more difficult to quantify. There's no easy way to measure how much you've healed emotionally from your past abuse or how effectively you're managing your abuser's ongoing attempts to hurt you. For this reason, focusing on taking practical steps forward toward rebuilding your finances and career can be a great source of confidence and motivation on your healing journey, since you can literally watch your progress and celebrate concrete goals as you reach them.

Most importantly, I hope you'll embrace the opportunities that lie ahead and give yourself permission to dream about a better future. It can be difficult to overcome hurtful things your abuser said to you, along with your own self-doubts and insecurities that arise as you work toward your goals. However, no matter what you experienced in the past, you are worthy of a brighter, more meaningful future, which includes financial stability and a sense of accomplishment. The world needs what you have to offer, which is a lot. Allow yourself to embrace this truth as you take each small step forward toward reclaiming a brighter future with respect to financial stability and educational and career success.

10
HELPING OTHERS

"I'm sharing my story with you because I want to help others."

We heard the sentiment reflected in the statement above so many times when we were doing our research related to the See the Triumph campaign. In fact, it was because so many survivors told us they wanted to help others that we decided to start See the Triumph in the first place. When we began our research, we were approaching the process as more traditional research, in that we hoped to learn from survivors who participated in our research, and then share our research findings in scholarly journal articles and conference presentations. That's what we were trained to do in graduate school and what we were paid to do in our work as university professors.

However, when we started listening to survivors' stories and their reasons for wanting to be a part of our research, we heard over and over again a deep desire to help others. It wasn't other researchers and professors they wanted to help. It *was* other survivors and other people at risk for abuse who were on their hearts to help. We knew scholarly journal articles and conference presentations wouldn't be an effective way to reach the people our research participants wanted to help. That's what led us to launch a social media campaign, so the words and experiences of survivors could more directly reach—and help—the people they wanted to reach.

Let me make clear from the beginning of this chapter that each survivor should be empowered to make their own decisions about whether they want to help others impacted by abuse. If you don't have any desire to help others facing or at risk for abuse, that is a perfectly valid decision. Some survivors would rather move forward in a way that doesn't involve revisiting their past experiences, so they decide to move away from any connections to the issue of abuse. That decision is understandable and valid. It doesn't mean you don't have a heart for others, and in fact, it's likely you have a heart for helping others, just in different ways and by focusing on other social issues that you're more passionate about. Don't let anyone make you feel shame or guilt because you're making the right choice for you and your personal healing process.

That being said, I've heard so many times from survivors that they desire deeply to help others—whether by educating younger generations about healthy relationships and red flags of abuse, offering support to someone currently facing abuse, or doing professional work to support victims and survivors on a daily basis. This desire to help others can serve as a powerful part of the healing process for survivors, for those who choose to take this path. As one example, read below to hear how finding ways to give back was a key part of the healing process for one of the survivors in our research:

> Abuse is wrong in any form. In my experience, I had to work on myself and question deeply why I considered it acceptable. In reality, I did not. Fear hijacked my mind; it was inseparable, until I stood up for myself. I then realized the men abusing me were in more fear than I was, even though it did not seem that way at the time. I have had a fixation problem always wanting better and seeing the good in the worst. Personally, for me, I had to refocus this energy to something of the greater good, I chose charity organizations. I had to find the acceptance of which I am, a person always willing to give the shirt off my back to help. I'm a helper. For me, I had to find the outlet that fulfills this need.

Helping others offers one way to make meaning of your past suffering. It allows you to take lessons you've learned through past difficulties and apply them in a way that makes a positive difference for others. You can feel a deep sense of satisfaction from helping others and knowing you've impacted their lives. Many survivors told us they were so grateful for the help, support, and encouragement they received from other survivors during their journey of recovering from past abuse, and they want to pay it forward by doing the same for others. Although it's not necessary to have personally experienced abuse to be able to offer support to someone who's facing abuse, people who've lived through the pain of abuse can draw upon their firsthand knowledge to offer a deep sense of validation for the experiences of others.

In my personal experience, I know I've been driven by a desire to help others. It's one of the ways that I've made meaning of my own experiences with abuse. When I look at those experiences just for the hurt they caused me, it's hard to understand why things happened the way they did. But, when I remind myself I had those experiences, have been on the healing journey from them, and can use them to inform my work to support survivors, teach people about healthy relationships, and advocate for community-level changes to better serve victims and survivors, I can see a greater purpose and meaning behind the difficult times I've had. I wouldn't wish those experiences on myself or anyone else, but I can see how they've uniquely positioned me to help others.

The same can be true for you! What are you uniquely positioned to do, or who are you uniquely positioned to help, based on your own experiences? There are many possible ways you can use your personal experiences to help others. The best way is what makes sense for you in your own life. For some, this means a career change to full-time work with victims of abuse. For others, it is more subtle, like being there for a friend or family member who's going through or recovering from an abusive relationship. In the remainder of this chapter, we'll explore some ways survivors can consider helping others, and then we'll look at considerations for determining when is the right time to begin helping others while you're in your own healing journey and how to build upon your own experiences in helping others, but also honor the uniqueness of each person's experiences.

Ways to Help Others

A lot of survivors have it in their hearts to help others but feel overwhelmed by the prospect of knowing just how to do so. Sometimes, opportunities present themselves naturally, such as if a friend or family member shares with you that they or someone close to them is in an abusive relationship and asks for your help. However, other opportunities need to be intentionally sought out. For these opportunities, survivors may not know where to start in finding ways to turn their desire to help others into actual steps toward doing so.

This section offers ideas for how you might begin exploring possible ways to put your passion for helping others into action. A lot of the ideas in this section come from a study[1] my colleagues and I did related to the See the Triumph campaign on how survivors of intimate partner violence see themselves as advocates for social change. In this study, we asked survivors to share their views about how they engage in advocacy-related activities to help others individually or at a community level. While advocacy activities are just one way people can help others, the lessons we learned through this research offer helpful insights for survivors considering ways to help others. Another potential way survivors can help others is by sharing their stories with them, and this topic is covered in Chapter 11 since storytelling is both a way to help others and a way to further promote one's own healing.

As someone who personally knows about what it's like to live through an abusive relationship, you've gained valuable life experiences that put you in a unique position to help others. Fortunately, there are many ways you could offer help to others, and in the research study I mentioned above, we found that there were both "big" and "small" ways survivors can offer help and support to others. I put "big" and "small" in quotes because even seemingly smaller ways of offering support can make a huge impact!

Of course, some survivors go on after an abusive relationship to dedicate their lives and careers to supporting other survivors, and that is a huge thing for someone to do. But, you can make a major difference in the lives of others even through seemingly smaller ways of offering help. For example, imagine if you shared one social media post with contact information for a local domestic violence agency, and a friend who's facing abuse saw your post and was inspired to reach out for help. Whether or not that friend ever tells you it was your post that led them to call the agency, your seemingly small act of sharing one piece of information on social media may have literally saved the life of your friend. The movement to end domestic and sexual violence will be a long one—every little bit of help and support that people provide can help make a big difference! Read on for more ideas of big and small ways you might consider offering help, support, and information to others. This section also offers tips for getting started with helping others in ways that are meaningful for you.

"Big" Ways to Help Others

We've heard many stories from survivors who participated in our research who became powerful advocates to help others. For example, several survivors shared that they became speakers to educate others in their community about intimate partner violence:

"My goal is to speak locally and statewide to churches and other organizations that commonly misguide women who are seeking refuge and help from abusive relationships."

"I share my story with women and teens to give them hope."

"I speak to others who are dealing with situations I dealt with. Also, [I] work with youth ministry that motivates teens to overcome hardships."

"I lecture around the country about the dynamics of IPV, surviving IPV, the generational cycle of family violence, and many other facets of this societal and criminal problem."

Other survivors even take on helping others as a career:

"I have been an advocate in my role as a nurse educator in a large women's clinic, mostly providing information and referrals."

"I am a proud survivor of domestic violence, and I am happy my work at the agency changed my career. I went from wanting to be a teacher to becoming a social worker and wanting to get a law degree and help abused immigrants with their immigration cases."

"Today I work … for a DV program … I love my job and frequently share my story with other women. The most gratifying thing I have ever heard is 'hearing your story today made me realize that I am a victim of domestic violence,' that woman's journey to freedom began that day. What a blessing!"

"I manage the [charitable work] for the company I work for where we donate a percentage of our sales to the NCADV to help end domestic violence. I have gone above and beyond what my job requires to help the NCADV and in turn help other women that have or are going through experiences probably much worse than mine. I hope to do much more in the near future."

"I am a full-time paid court advocate for a DV shelter. I had always worked in the legal field and discovered that I really enjoyed working with victims of crime, specifically DV. I have been doing direct services for 5 years and plan on making a career of it."

Some advocates turn to social media to raise awareness about intimate partner violence, such as the following survivors in our research:

> "I run a Facebook page and have 1000 followers. I want to grow the page much larger."

> "I've also helped run DV pages on Facebook that help women once they leave."

> "I am admin on a Facebook page, our numbers are growing and growing."

Helping others also can look like community-building efforts in your local community. For example, one survivor in our research said, "I started in college, after I'd gotten some therapy on my own, sharing my story with others, and taking steps to help my friends stay out of trouble. And a little network began to grow and never stopped. I now know lots of people who have experienced some sort of trauma and lots of resources to help people deal with them. I've learned that everyone has something that hurts them and by sharing it we all become stronger." Another said, "I now head up a ... group within our church for single parents. We will be working within this group for family violence and adding programs for them also."

Efforts to help others also may take the form of working with organizations to ensure they are best meeting the needs of survivors. As one example, a research study participant said, "I have assisted law enforcement in writing policies for effective law enforcement response to domestic violence, testifying as an expert witness in civil and criminal cases."

For those interested in learning how to become an advocate, many local domestic violence agencies offer formal advocacy trainings. These classes can be valuable, as one participant in our research said, "I'm taking classes to become an advocate. I want to help change the system that is so broken. I want to help other women." A good place to start in seeing if a program like this exists in your community is by connecting with your state domestic violence coalition or a local domestic violence service agency.

When it comes to advocacy, don't be afraid to dream big! Intimate partner violence is such a major problem in society that we need people to advocate for creative solutions that will promote real changes toward ending abuse. For example, one survivor in our research shared her dream with us: "My dream now is to make an organization to help women like myself to have resources, tools and the guidance to how to get out, help them with housing, work placement, and childcare: Everything that I never had."

I hope these "big" examples inspire you to consider how you might start or continue being part of large-scale efforts to help others and promote change in your own community and beyond! However, as I mentioned earlier, I hope you'll also consider the major impact that even seemingly "smaller" types of offering help and support can make a huge impact, which we'll discuss further in the next section.

"Small" Ways to Help Others

Smaller-scale efforts to help others are just as valuable as larger-scale efforts, and even though they may be viewed as "smaller" than more major efforts, they can deliver huge impacts for individuals and communities.

One of the simplest things anyone can do to advocate for survivors is simply to listen to their stories when you have the opportunity. For example, one survivor in our research said, "I will be there when someone needs me." Another said, "I simply try to be there for friends/acquaintances who are in abusive relationships." Given what we know about how isolated survivors can become through abuse, just think how powerful being there and listening can be.

Beyond listening to survivors' stories, survivors especially can help others by sharing their own experiences to help other survivors know that they aren't alone. We'll talk more about sharing your story in the next chapter, but for now, you can see in the following quotes from research study participants just how much they viewed this as a key way they could offer support to others:

"I have reached out to close friends who have been in similar situations to share with them."

"I've given people advice sometimes but only if they ask. I know what they are going through ... the fear ... the pain ... the disbelief in their self ... I always try and help someone out of a situation if I can."

"Speaking about my abusive past is something that I HAVE done with close friends that were in the beginning phases of partner violence. I have helped a few of them remove themselves from those situations."

"I will try to offer advice or help if I know someone is in a bad relationship."

Another way to offer help and advocate to end abuse is to speak up about the topic in everyday conversations to ensure others have accurate information and understand the challenges survivors face. For example, one participant in our research said, "Anytime I hear anyone speaking about domestic violence, I speak up and take up for the women. I have had people say if they stay after they have been hit, then they deserve it. I told them they need to go look up the statistics on how many women end up dead because they just leave." Another said, "I talk about my experience every chance I get, in the hopes that someone within earshot will be encouraged to get help and get away." Another participant said simply, "I speak out against abuse."

In my discussion above on "big" ways of offering help, I shared how some people start new social media campaigns or run Facebook pages. However, social media offers people opportunities for raising awareness about abuse through less-intensive actions, too. For example, a research participant said, "I share posts, articles, etc., on Facebook and Twitter and Pinterest."

Some people truly feel called and motivated to take on large-scale efforts to help others, and these efforts are commendable. But remember that even ways of helping others that seem "small" can make a big difference! You may provide a listening ear to someone who's experiencing abuse, which could help start the process for them to leave the relationship and change the course of their lives forever. You could share your own experiences with abuse and let someone know they're not alone, and that there is hope. You could share a piece of information with someone in your social media network that helps them recognize an abusive relationship in their own life and start to take action to get safe. Small actions can have big results.

Getting Started

As we've seen throughout this section, there are many big and small ways survivors can channel their desire to help others into meaningful actions that make a difference in the lives of others. Helping others means different things to different people, so one of the first steps is to think about what ways of helping would be most meaningful to you. Consider the following questions:

- What social issues related to abuse do you feel most strongly about?
- What skills, resources, and connections do you have already that you could build on to help others?
- What unique insights or experiences can you share with others to make a difference?

Some people want to help others but don't know how to go about it. For example, one participant in our research said, "I do not see myself as an advocate but I think I could be and I would be interested in how to become one." Another said, "I don't know if I have the skills." If that sounds like you, consider if you might begin by joining efforts with others, such as your local domestic violence agency or another local or online group. Many organizations value the energy and skills that volunteers bring, and they may offer training and volunteer opportunities to help you develop your skills and confidence so that you could take on other ways of helping others in the future.

Survivors in our research shared some of the knowledge and skills they thought were beneficial in their efforts to help others, and the following quotes provide examples of these:

> "Listen carefully, be gentle and let the other person take her own pace."
>
> "You have to learn the laws, understand your role/liability and be responsible for the consequences of your actions."
>
> "You need to know cyber-safety and how to keep your family safe."
>
> "You have to know accurate information."
>
> "I am a writer and I would like to write about abusive relationships and situations to expose what few people realize is going on behind the cover of darkness, shame and fear."

It also can be helpful to have realistic expectations about how advocacy efforts may be received. For example, one participant had this to say about her efforts to help others:

> The biggest skill you need is to be ok with people looking at you funny/uncomfortably. You have to deal with not being welcomed and learn how to deliver horrendously toxic information in a receptive way. You have to learn to face extreme hostility and not be reactive but responsive.

Violence and abuse aren't easy topics for many people to discuss, and this quote is a great reminder of how important it is to understand how these topics may be received by your target audience.

Helping others may be a life-long process, and there will likely be times when you feel more or less motivated to help. Along with the excitement and satisfaction that can come with progress, helping others can be wrought with frustration, stress, and even anger. Keeping a long-range perspective and staying focused on the importance of the end goal to end abuse can help buffer you against frustrations that may arise. It's also important to consider ways to help others while honoring and caring for yourself and your own healing journey, which we'll discuss further in the next section.

Helping Others While Honoring Yourself

Two important considerations before and during opportunities you might take on with the intention of helping others are first, focusing on your own healing as you consider when is the right time to help others, and second, understanding how to draw upon your own experiences while also honoring each survivor's unique experiences.

When Is the Right Time to Help?

For many survivors, the healing and recovery process can become a lifelong journey. Therefore, being completely healed (if there is such a thing) isn't a prerequisite for helping others, and survivors can begin to explore opportunities to help others even while they're working on their own healing journey. On the other hand, if someone's wounds are fresh, and they're oozing hurt and pain out of their pores, they're probably not in the best position to help others. Just like we're instructed on an airplane to put on our own oxygen mask first before helping others, we can best position ourselves to help others by first helping ourselves along our own healing journey.

Somewhere in between "completely healed" and oozing pain is where most survivors find themselves when they seek out or are presented with opportunities to help others. It's important to be far enough along in your healing journey before focusing much of your time and energy on helping others. Trying to help others before you've focused on your own healing first can lead you to expend valuable energy and time on others that could be better used to support your own healing. And, helping others while your wounds are still fresh could be re-traumatizing for you as you vicariously experience their hurts through your interactions with them.

I encourage you to think carefully about when to focus on helping others, especially if it diverts your attention and focus away from your own healing process. Some people find it possible to both be focusing on their own healing and also offering help to others, but for others, the toll that helping others takes might be too difficult to bear. There are no right or wrong answers here. And, since the abuse recovery journey can be an unpredictable one, especially if you face ongoing abuse or other contact with your former abuser, it's possible you may go through phases when you feel ready to help others, then you need to take time off to focus on your own healing, and back and forth while you go through different phases of the recovery process.

Any time you're presented with or are considering opportunities to help others, it's wise to ask yourself, "How might this opportunity impact my own healing journey?" Know it's okay and healthy to acknowledge if you're not in a position to help, and in those cases, it can be helpful to offer the person, people, or organization who need help suggestions for other resources where they can turn for help, such as a local domestic violence service agency. Sometimes, when I find I'm not in a position to take on an opportunity I've been given, I will answer by saying, "I'm sorry I can't take this on now, but please keep me in mind if similar opportunities come up in the future." Setting these boundaries can be healthy for you, as well as allow the other person, people, or organization to get help from another source.

To help decide whether you're in a position to consider helping others, below are some signs that you may or may not be ready:

Signs that It May Not Be the Right Time to Take On Helping Others

- You have active symptoms of PTSD, and the experiences of others might trigger panic or other symptoms for you.
- You're facing ongoing abuse.
- You're currently in the middle of legal processes involving your abuser.
- You lack adequate social support (e.g., friends, family members, or a professional counselor) to help you if you face difficult, intense emotions while helping others.
- You're still overwhelmed by making sense of your own experiences, which may make it difficult to separate your experiences from the experiences of others.
- You don't have strong coping skills in place.

Signs that You May Be Ready to Take On Opportunities to Help Others

- You have spent a good bit of time on self-reflection about your experiences with abuse.
- You have developed a solid set of coping skills and resources.
- You have learned about the patterns and dynamics of abusive relationships.

- You have a strong desire to help others.
- You have a strong enough sense of self-worth and could handle rejection or other people not listening to you, not acting kindly toward you, or not following your guidance or suggestions.
- You're open to learning new skills and information to help you help others more effectively.
- You can build upon your own emotions and experiences, but also honor the unique journey that each person is on.
- You're able to manage your emotions so that, if you do become emotionally overwhelmed when helping others, you can work through those emotions in a constructive way so that they won't get in the way of your ability to help others.

The above lists are just a starting point for you to consider whether or not you're currently in a position to help others. You may have other unique circumstances that make it more or less likely that helping others could become a hindrance to your own healing process. Also, consider the nature of different possible ways to help others. Even if you may not be ready to take on more emotionally-intense opportunities to help (such as providing close support to a good friend who is leaving an abusive partner), you might still be able to find ways to help others that are less intense, yet still meaningful for you. For example, you might consider making a small donation to a local domestic violence agency as one way to give back while you work toward being ready to take on more intense ways to help, such as becoming a crisis line volunteer at that same agency.

Making decisions about whether and when to help others is an ongoing process. You may start offering help, but then realize you're becoming overwhelmed, so decide to take a few steps back. Continue to focus on building self-awareness, as well as understanding how changing circumstances around you might impact your ability to help. It's always wise to practice self-care while caring for others.

How to Build on Your Own Experiences *and* Honor Each Person's Unique Experiences

Another unique consideration for survivors who are interested in helping others is finding the balance between drawing from the wisdom you gained from your experiences while also honoring the fact that others' experiences are naturally going to differ from your own. To be able to help others effectively, it's important to value the uniqueness in each person's experiences. If you don't do this, you may offer advice or support in a way that would have been helpful for you, but may not be the most helpful for them.

While it's true there are common patterns and dynamics in abusive relationships, these play out in different ways in different relationships. In addition to the dynamics of the abuse, many other factors can influence a person's experiences with abuse, such as how much social support they have, their income level, their cultural background, and their values about relationships and families. Because each person's life experiences are so unique, it's wise to assume that even though you've faced a similar life experience of abuse, there are many differences between your and others' experiences. One useful question to keep in mind when offering support to another person who has faced abuse is, *How is my experience similar and different as compared to this person's experiences?* Keep those similarities and differences in mind as you consider how to offer to help and support them.

Another useful question to consider, and often to ask directly is, *What does this person/community/organization need from me right now?* Some people simply need someone to listen to them. Another person may benefit from learning insights about what life is like on the inside of an abusive relationship. Still others need to gain new knowledge about the dynamics of abuse, practical advice to navigate a specific situation, or even tangible support, such as financial assistance or support with child care or transportation. Take time to truly understand the needs of others, and adjust your approach to helping to address their unique needs.

If you decide to share some of your own experiences with abuse as part of your efforts to help others, be mindful of the impact of your self-disclosure on the other person. When I was in graduate school for counseling, one of the first lessons we learned was to be very careful about self-disclosure. We may be sharing our experiences to try to help another person know we understand their experiences, but in fact disclosures may be off-putting to some people if they feel you're focusing on your experiences and not listening fully to theirs. If you choose to self-disclose some of your experiences, try to carefully observe how the other person responds. You may find they seem excited or relieved to know they're not alone. On the other hand, you also may find they seem to shut down if they don't see how your experiences connect with their own experiences.

One way to increase your ability to connect your own experiences with others' experiences is by continuing to educate yourself about the dynamics of abuse and how it can manifest differently for different people and populations. It can be especially useful to learn how different social or cultural backgrounds can impact experiences of abuse. Keep in mind traumatic experiences are individualized and dependent on how the person facing the trauma perceives it. This is one reason why it's so important to avoid comparing experiences. Experiences that seem minor to one person could seem major to others, and vice versa. When considering how you can build upon your experiences with abuse to help others, remember to honor each person's unique experiences—including your own and the people you aim to help—and work together through a collaborative approach to figure out how you can best be of help in any given situation.

Conclusion

Helping others can be an extremely meaningful part of the abuse recovery process. Of course, helping others isn't a necessary step to heal, and each survivor should be empowered to make decisions for themselves about whether, when, and how to focus on helping others, especially with respect to how it might impact their own healing journey. If the desire to help others is in your heart, then consider "big" and "small" ways you might bring that desire to life. By helping others, you may find opportunities to transform the hurts of your past into making a positive impact on others. Of course, most survivors probably wish the abuse they faced had never happened. However, using your past hurts as fuel for your passion to help others can help you feel more at peace as you come to terms with your experiences and see some good as coming from those experiences.

Helping others also can offer new opportunities for healing, especially if challenging memories or emotions rise to the surface in the process of helping others. As you work through these opportunities, you can move toward even greater levels of healing, although of course it's important to ensure your own healing is not coming at the expense of others. Take good care of yourself while you're helping and caring for others. By continuing to focus on your own healing, it's likely you'll find even more doors opening to even greater opportunities to help others. Honor and value your own lived experiences with abuse, while also honoring and valuing the unique and different experiences with others. Build upon the resources in your Coping Toolkit to help you stay refreshed and recharged along the way!

Reference

1   Murray, C. E., King, K., Crowe, A., & Flasch, P. (2015). Survivors of intimate partner violence as advocates for social change. *Journal of Social Action in Counseling and Psychology, 7*, 84–100. https://openjournals.bsu.edu/jsacp/article/view/353

11

TELLING YOUR STORY, ON YOUR OWN TERMS

"I found my voice again. I started to write about what happened to me. I started speaking out and becoming active on social media about domestic violence. I will never not have a voice again. Other people's discomfort with my voice is their issue, not mine."

~ Domestic Violence Survivor

There's a Native American proverb that says, "It takes a thousand voices to tell a single story." I've always loved this proverb in the context of the stories of survivors of abuse. Each individual survivor has their own unique story, and there are many common themes that cut across all survivors' stories. To fully tell the collective story of what it means to live through, heal from, and triumph over abusive relationships, we need to create spaces for individual survivors to share their stories in ways that are meaningful to them.

Stories hold power. *Your* story holds power. It holds power to educate and inform others. Your story can challenge other people's ways of thinking. And your story holds potential to help others heal. That said, there are no right or wrong ways to tell your story. Some survivors share their stories publicly in large, open forums or in the media. Others share their stories with just a few close confidants. Still others find release by simply writing their own story in a journal. You may choose a combination of these ways at different points in your journey. What's most important is to be empowered to decide whether, why, how, when, and to whom to tell your story, and this chapter aims to help you think through those decisions.

Reasons to Tell Your Story

Your story matters. Telling your story, on your own terms, can be an important part of your healing journey, as well as a way to help others, as discussed in the last chapter. The experiences you've had matter. Your story is as individual as you are. This section focuses on reasons survivors can benefit from telling their stories: the power of owning your story, gaining control of your memories, helping and inspiring others, and raising awareness about abuse.

Owning Your Story

Claiming your story — including your "big picture" story and all the smaller stories within it — is empowering. By "big picture" story, I mean the overarching story of your experiences with abuse and your healing journey. Even though I use the term "smaller" to describe more detailed, intricate stories of your day-to-day (or even moment-to-moment) experiences within that bigger picture story, the smaller stories can have a big impact. For example, I can share the overarching story that having been abused is part of my life experiences, and that overall story has meaning for me and others who may hear it. But, I could also tell you some of the nitty-gritty details of specific things that happened as part of that relationship, down to details of where I was, what was said, and how I felt in the moment. That level of detail holds a lot of power and meaning, too.

Most survivors would probably need days, weeks, or even months to share all aspects of their stories! They could tell the story of how their abuser pursued them and gained their trust. They could tell the story of the first time the abuser hurt them and how the abuser acted afterward. And then, there are probably many, many other stories of abusive actions done over time and how abuse started to impact their feelings about themselves and the relationship. To add to that, survivors carry other stories of how professionals, friends, and family members responded to them when they disclosed their abuse. There are also stories of when and how the relationship ended, along with the story of the recovery process that followed.

I hope the above list of possible aspects of survivors' stories feels exciting and not overwhelming. You have a lot of stories to tell, and you get to decide which stories to share with others, which to keep to yourself, and how to tell them. Now, if the thought of telling your story feels overwhelming or scary, keep in mind you're probably telling your story already. Chances are, even if you're not consciously doing it, you're already telling your stories, possibly many times each day! This may be happening only in your mind as you replay memories of abuse or your recovery process. As we discussed earlier in this book, PTSD is a common experience for survivors, and even when there's not a PTSD diagnosis, replaying memories of past experiences is common for survivors. Avoiding those memories also is common, but chances are memories of past abuse slip into your mind from time to time, and likely even more often than that.

Gaining Control of Your Memories

One reason storytelling can be so powerful for survivors is because *intentionally* telling and retelling your story, on your own terms, can help you regain control of your memories. It's common as a trauma survivor to experience triggers, or things that bring old memories back to the surface. Typically, these triggers aren't things you choose and often can come to your attention in surprising ways. It may be a song on the radio, passing by a location where a significant event played out, or even certain smells. When those memories replay as stories in your mind, they can offer insights and clues to help you on your healing journey. On the other hand, simply allowing them to replay over and over again can cause distress, rather than insight. If you've ever found yourself replaying circumstances from past abuse and getting upset in the process, then you know what I'm talking about.

Intentional storytelling helps you realize there are many possible ways you could describe the story of any given incident. For example, if I'm telling the story of why I chose to stay in my past relationship even when I realized the hurt it was causing me, I could tell it in a way that makes me look weak, or I could tell it in another way that highlights the strength it took me to be building myself up and planning during that time for ending the relationship when I was ready. Often when it comes to the complex circumstances involved in life with an abuser, there are many layers to every situation, and multiple "truths" can be true at once. How you tell your stories, and possibly even refine them over time, can reflect your healing journey and your path toward overcoming past abuse. Intentional efforts to tell your story can help you realize parts of your story you didn't notice before, particularly as you share the strength and power you displayed while overcoming difficult past experiences.

Helping and Inspiring Others

In the last chapter, we focused on ways survivors can help others. Sharing your story offers a powerful way you can help others. Sometimes, all someone facing or recovering from abuse needs to know is they're not alone and not the only one who has gone through abuse. Often, if your aim is to help others, you don't even need to go into much detail to be able to make an impact. It can be enough to simply say, "I've been in a similar situation, and I know how hard it is." Remember how lonely and embarrassing it can feel when you're in or just coming out of a relationship with an abuser. Just hearing you're not alone can touch deeply in your soul.

Your story also can inspire others when they can see themselves in your journey, especially if they see you're in the process of overcoming abuse and going on to build a happy, safe life. You don't have to be at the end of the journey (if there even is such a thing!) to make this impact. In fact, survivors' stories often can make the most impact on others when they reveal the journey is still in progress. Isn't it refreshing to find out people who you view as having their act together are still a work in progress, too? When you share your past and current progress with others, you show them it's possible to move toward healing, as well as inspire them to believe in their ability to do the same thing.

Raising Awareness about Abuse

Stories are important for educating people about the dynamics of abusive relationships and countering common stereotypes about abuse. For example, many people without personal experience of abuse often wonder why people stay in abusive relationships. However, when they hear stories of how hard it is to leave an abuser, it can open their eyes to the truth and debunk the stereotype that people who stay in abusive relationships are weak or somehow want to be abused. In the public sphere, it's important that stories from survivors of all different backgrounds are highlighted to show that abuse can happen to virtually anybody.

Survivors' stories also can inform public policy and community decision-making. Statistics and data are often used to make decisions at this level. However, numbers don't tell the whole story of the lived experiences of people who've walked through abuse, especially as they relate to public and organizational policies that impact resources survivors can access in communities. Survivors' stories are especially useful for highlighting barriers in systems and organizations that should be set up to help victims and survivors. Although not every survivor wants to bring their story into the public sphere, it's important that communities build forums for survivors to share their stories (including anonymously) to help bring abuse into the light. Abuse thrives in darkness and silence, when people falsely hold onto viewpoints that abuse doesn't happen or that it happens to only certain types of people. By bringing survivors' stories into the light—and into the public sphere for those who choose to share their stories in this way—powerful steps are taken toward overcoming the silence that allows abuse to persist.

Deciding Whether to Tell Your Story Publicly

Despite the potential benefits to telling your story, remember you have the power to make choices about whether and how telling your story is right for you, now and at any time in the future. Based on research I've done, my counseling and community work, and my own personal experiences, I'm convinced private storytelling (such as writing in a journal or talking with a counselor, support group, or close friends) can have benefits for nearly all survivors. However, this section will focus on public forms of storytelling, including anything from sharing your story with one person or small groups of people you don't know well to speaking at public awareness events and to the media. Public storytelling isn't right for all survivors, and certainly not right for everyone all the time. This section is designed to help you think through important considerations if you're thinking about sharing your story publicly.

You don't have to publicly share your story to be a "successful" or "fully healed" survivor of abuse. Certainly, there are many possible benefits for survivors who share their stories publicly, as well as for others who hear those public stories. However, there's no rule you must share your story publicly in any way. In fact, there are no rules of any kind about telling your story or identifying as a survivor to anyone other than yourself. Of course, as we've discussed throughout this book, it's wise to seek out the right kinds of help from others—such as counselors, victim advocates, close friends and family members, and others—to support you along your recovery journey. However, you can be empowered to decide whether, when, how, and to whom you tell your story in ways that are right for you.

This was a difficult lesson for me to learn personally. For many years before I publicly shared that I, too, had personal experiences of abuse, my work had been focused on research, teaching, practice, and community advocacy related to domestic and sexual abuse, as well as other forms of family and interpersonal violence. I had to work through feelings of being hypocritical that I was doing this work but not being open publicly about my own experiences. I've always been open with close friends and family members about what I'd gone through, but my identity as a survivor wasn't something I publicly brought into my work. Of course, what I learned through my personal experiences was a driving force for the passion I brought to my work, but I didn't yet bring my story out into the open in public spheres related to my work.

What I realized after struggling with this decision for a long time was that I wasn't required to publicly share my story just because I worked in this field. Although there was a part of me that looked forward to the day when I could be more open about my experiences, the reasons I was choosing not to publicly share my story outweighed the reasons I would have wanted to do so. Two of those reasons included fears for my safety and parenting concerns, in that I wanted to wait until my children were old enough that I could talk with them privately about my identity as a survivor before they might potentially hear about it from someone else first if I shared my story publicly.

For anyone trying to decide if they should share all or parts of their story of abuse publicly, it's important to think this decision through carefully to weigh all the potential risks and benefits. Through our See the Triumph social media campaign, we often connect with survivors who want to volunteer as guest bloggers for the campaign. Providing this platform for survivors to share their stories has been one of my favorite aspects of the campaign, so we're always excited to offer this opportunity to prospective bloggers. However, we always make sure to talk through the decision whether to attach guest bloggers' names and photos to their posts, because we want to make sure that would be safe and comfortable for them to do so. We offer options to run survivors' posts anonymously, with a pseudonym, with their partial name (i.e., just a first name), or with their full name. By providing options, we hope to empower survivors to choose the safest and most appropriate way to share their story at that point in their recovery journey.

Consider the following questions to help decide whether any public form of storytelling is right for you:

- *Is it safe for me to publicly share my story?* Safety concerns should always be a top priority when deciding whether to share your story publicly. Abusers can be very dangerous, and safety risks often continue long after an abusive relationship ends. Before you consider sharing your story publicly, evaluate whether your safety is at risk in any way. This includes your physical, emotional, mental, and financial safety. A good question to ask yourself is: *What might my former abuser do if they find out I shared my story in this way?* Might they retaliate with physical violence? Begin to threaten or harass you? Serve you with a defamation lawsuit? If there are any potential safety risks, it's important to think these through and potentially seek professional guidance, such as from an attorney, before speaking publicly.

- *If I share my experiences publicly, how much detail do I want to disclose? Is there a way for me to publicly identify as a survivor but still keep some details private?* There are ways you can share parts of your experiences publicly but still keep aspects of your experiences or identity private. Examples include using a pseudonym, as we offer to prospective See the Triumph bloggers, and talking in general terms and not disclosing any specific details that would identify your abuser, which is the approach I've chosen to take personally. Speaking in general terms can be tricky, however, because you have to consider whether people hearing your story could figure out who you're talking about based on what they know about you. Recently, we were talking with a potential See the Triumph blogger who was in her early 20s and had only one serious prior relationship, so anyone who knew her would know who she was talking about if she shared that she previously was involved with an abusive partner. For older survivors who've had different relationship experiences, it may be possible to talk more generally, such as by saying, "When I was abused in a former relationship ...", and nobody would be able to tell the relationship you're referencing without additional identifying details. If you decide to share your story in public forums, consider what level of detail is right for you. Keep in mind: Opening the book on your story of past abuse doesn't require you to open it the whole way! You can keep parts of the book closed and open only those parts you want to share with others.

- *Is this specific public platform right for me right now?* Public storytelling can take many forms, such as speaking at a local awareness event, giving a guest lecture at a local college or university, blogging, posting on social media, and doing a news interview for a newspaper, TV show, radio, or magazine. Each public platform has unique risks and opportunities, so weigh these carefully if you're thinking about venturing into a new forum for sharing your story. Of course, any time you share publicly in any way, you run a risk of losing control of your story, and you cannot control what others will say or do in response to your story. If you have any hesitations at all about a platform, consider all possible scenarios you can think of that may be upsetting or uncomfortable for you, and consider if you're up for handling them.

Having done a lot of public speaking myself, as well as having worked with many survivors around sharing their stories in different ways, I've seen firsthand some of the potential opportunities and risks that different public platforms offer. Here are just a few to consider for each of the ones listed above:

Speaking at Community Awareness Events

These events offer the potential to reach large numbers of people, most of whom likely chose to attend, so you can assume they have some level of interest in the issue. Usually, these events are relatively controlled, and there's generally not a question and answer period, so you're not too likely to face unexpected, offensive questions publicly. In many cases, speakers at these events have opportunities to talk with people from the audience after they're done talking, and in my experience people who approach someone who's just shared a story of abuse are often very appreciative and sometimes even share their own experiences with abuse. Of course, these events have some risks, too. Those risks may include hecklers or protestors, an inability to predict who'll be in the audience, and the potential you'll be video-recorded giving your talk, and you won't necessarily know how that video will be used. For example: Will they share it on social media or send it to friends? Thus, even if you're considering talking at a relatively controlled public awareness event, be mindful that what you say could end up online, in the news, or in some other much more public forum.

Giving a Lecture at a Local College or University

Having taught many university courses during my time as a professor, I know how powerful a learning experience it is for students to learn from survivors. By sharing your story with students, you could inspire them to make a difference in their future careers, as well as help them be equipped with greater knowledge if they or someone they know faces abuse in the future.

Classroom speaking is also a relatively controlled environment, and you can be relatively assured (if you request this) the students won't be recording your talk, and the instructor can help monitor this. One of the biggest risks to prepare for when speaking with students is the likelihood of uninformed questions that could feel blaming, hurtful, or offensive. Classroom instructors often encourage question and answer sessions, and I've witnessed even well-meaning students ask questions with an overt victim-blaming tone. So, if this speaking platform seems like a good fit for you, be ready to answer students' questions in a way that's educational, supportive, and corrective of inaccurate stereotypical views.

Blogging or Posting on Social Media

With so many blogging and social media platforms readily available today, the possibilities for sharing your story through these channels is endless. However, there are two main ways these technology-based platforms allow you to share your story—publicly or privately to a more limited audience you choose. However, even a "private" personal social media post has the potential to be shared, copied, or otherwise disclosed by someone in your network (such as if someone takes a screenshot of it and shares it with others), so be mindful of privacy considerations of any electronic forms of telling your story. Also keep in mind that once something is on the Internet, it can live on virtually forever. So, use caution and be sure to think through possible safety and privacy considerations any time you choose to share your story online.

Doing News Interviews for Newspapers, TV, Radio, or Magazines

Mass media interviews can be very exciting—and very daunting. You have the potential to reach a huge audience through these platforms, which has advantages and disadvantages. Of course, the more people you reach, the more people you have the potential to impact with your story. On the other hand, the broader audience might carry increased safety risks, especially if your abuser finds out about the story. Many media outlets offer the option of sharing your story anonymously or in disguise (such as a TV interview that doesn't show the speaker's face and distorts their voice). However, when your identity is attached to a media story, keep in mind that media stories can live on indefinitely through the Internet. Consider that anyone, such as a future employer, might find your story if they search for you online. Media interviews have potential to reach a lot of people, so be sure to think through whether you're ready for this level of public sharing before sharing your story if you have the chance to speak to the media.

Am I Ready to Face the Stigma of Publicly Identifying as a Survivor of Abuse?

Ideally, we would live in a world in which there would be no stigma attached to being a survivor of abuse. In this ideal world, only people who abuse others would face stigma, judgment, and blame, and survivors would receive the admiration and celebration they deserve for their strength and courage. While the world has changed a good deal as more survivors have come forward with their stories, unfortunately many people still hold negative stereotypes and stigmatizing beliefs. If you take the bold risk of sharing your story publicly, chances are you'll encounter some people who will view you negatively because of your experiences. You may start to wonder if people are talking about you behind your back, and they just might be. Your disclosure could become fodder for gossip. Others may make comments to you to your face that seem hurtful, offensive, or victim-blaming. While these comments can become an opportunity to educate others, you may grow tired of facing these comments and reactions.

The focus of this book has been on empowering you to make the best decisions for yourself in your journey of recovering from and triumphing over abuse. Some of you may have read the above paragraph and thought, "Who cares what other people think?" Others may have read the same paragraph and thought, "I'd never want to deal with that sort of thing!" As I've emphasized throughout the book, the choice is yours to make about whether facing the risk of public stigma is something you want to take on. I've spoken with survivors who find facing stigma head-on by sharing their story publicly is an important part of their healing process. On the other hand, I've met other survivors who found the stigma to be an unexpected, exhausting part of publicly sharing their identity as a survivor. Until there's no more stigma surrounding the experience of being abused, it's important to acknowledge the stigma exists as you make choices about whether and how to share your story.

What Are the Potential Risks and Benefits of Telling My Story?

Each question in this section was designed to help you explore different facets of the choice to share your story publicly. In addition, a basic risk/benefit analysis can be helpful. This may be as simple as taking out a piece of paper, drawing a line down the middle of the paper, writing "Risks" and "Benefits" on each side of the paper, and then making a list on each side. Even this simple process helps bring clarity when making big decisions. Don't just look at the number of items on each list—it may be there's one big risk or benefit that outweighs a lot of smaller risks or benefits on the other side. Pay attention to your emotions while making your lists, and know it's okay to trust your intuition to make the best decision for you at this time.

How to Tell Your Story

Once you've made decisions about whether to share your story publicly, privately, or both ways, it's time to start exploring specific strategies for storytelling that can help you take steps forward on your healing journey. The most basic answer to the question of, "I'd like to start telling my story, but where do I start?" is: "Any way you decide is right for you!" To help get started, this section covers different ways to share and express your story.

Private Forms of Storytelling

Below are ideas for private ways to share your story.

Informal Journal Writing

Grab a notebook and start putting your pen to the paper. Since this journal is for your eyes only, just let your story pour out, and don't worry how clear it is, whether you've got proper grammar, or even if you can read your handwriting if it's messy. Try writing out your story overall, as well as smaller, more detailed stories of specific incidents within your overall story.

More Structured Forms of Writing

Explore different writing styles, such as writing poetry, writing your story in third-person language, telling the story as you imagine it from the perspective of different people (e.g., you, your children, or your best friend), writing about your dreams, and letter-writing.

Artistic Storytelling

You can free yourself from limitations of language by bringing creative arts to the storytelling process. Any form of art that resonates with you can be used as a platform for telling your story, such as visual arts, music, and even doodling! Check out our free See the Triumph Healing Arts Workshops guide for some creative art projects that might be useful in this process: www.seethetriumph.org/see-the-triumph-healing-arts-workshops.html.

Speaking with a Confidential Professional, such as a Counselor or Faith Leader

Sharing your story with a trained professional can be a powerful experience, both for your healing and for clarifying your story to potentially one day share with others. I've touched on the benefits of counseling in other places throughout this book, but it's important to add here the value of speaking with professionals as a channel for storytelling. An understanding, well-trained professional can help you sort through complicated or confusing aspects of your story, making this an interactive form of storytelling. A professional who's been trained in the specific therapy modality, Narrative Therapy, can be especially useful here, as Narrative Therapy focuses on helping clients explore and re-write the stories they tell about their life and experiences. *Psychology Today* offers an online directory to identify a therapist trained in Narrative Therapy in your area: www.psychologytoday.com/us/therapy-types/narrative-therapy.

Public Forms of Storytelling

Telling your story "publicly" can mean many different things. As discussed earlier, it's important to think through any possible safety risks that may be involved. There are many options for sharing your story with others publicly that can build on your interests, skills, and goals for sharing your story. For example, if you enjoy writing, you may try sharing your story through blogging, writing a book or essay, or writing letters to an editor or an op-ed for your local newspaper. If you're an artist, you may consider doing pieces that could be shared in a gallery or exhibit. Some people are terrified of public speaking, while other people love getting in front of a crowd. The same goes for media interviews, but these too can be a great platform for sharing your story with the public. One great way to get started with public speaking and media interviews is to connect with your local domestic violence agency to let them know of your interest. These organizations often are asked if they know of survivors who are willing to share their story, and some even offer trainings for building your skills in these areas, such as the See the Triumph Survivor Advocacy Training Program that we developed and offer as a free resource through our website: www.seethetriumph.org/see-the-triumph-survivor-advocacy-training-program.html. In addition, other ways you could develop new skills to help you with public forms of storytelling include taking a writing workshop, joining a class on public speaking, or joining a club like Toastmasters. As always, consider your privacy for any forms of public story-sharing, and explore whether there are ways to do so anonymously or by using a pseudonym if you're interested in sharing your story but not ready to connect your story to your name and identity.

When to Tell Your Story

One of the biggest questions you may struggle with as you consider different ways of telling your story of surviving abuse is, "Am I ready for this?" Ultimately, this is a question only you can answer, but I'll offer suggestions below to consider as you answer that question. First, there's no rule for the perfect time in your healing journey to start telling your story. You may find different types of storytelling are helpful to you at different points along that journey. Private types of storytelling can be valuable from the earliest stages of your journey. However, if you're currently involved with an abusive partner, be cautious about the safety implications of any forms of storytelling that you do, even privately. For example, if you're writing your story down in a personal journal or on a computer, consider whether your abuser could access what you've written.

Sharing your story publicly can bring up more risks than private storytelling, so the timing of any steps you take in that area should be carefully considered. With public storytelling, it's wise to wait until you've done some emotional healing work so you can feel confident and composed to face unexpected challenges that may arise. For example, with public speaking, remember you could face some sort of heckler or a person asking seemingly-rude questions, and you'd want to be able to respond in a confident, non-reactive way. It's harder to do that if you're still reeling from the emotional trauma of the abuse.

Here's a useful four-step strategy to use if you're considering if it's the right time to share your story in any new way, whether publicly or even just telling a new friend in private:

• First, ask yourself: "What is the absolute worst thing that could happen if I tell my story in this way?" It's possible a few potential negative outcomes could come to mind.

- Second, for each one that comes to mind, ask yourself another question: "How would I feel if that thing happened? How would that feeling affect me?" For example, if you'd feel upset and angry but think you could work through those feelings with relative ease, it may still be worth taking that risk of sharing your story at that time. If, on the other hand, you'd be devastated if a friend rejected you or someone asked a rude question in a public speaking situation, it might be wise to continue working on your emotional healing and sense of self-worth before sharing your story in that way.
- Third, consider the following question: "Even if there are negative things that could happen, do I still feel ready for this?" You might view overcoming these risks as an important next step in your healing journey and decide it's the right timing to move forward despite them.
- And fourth, ask yourself if the timing is right based on whether you have the support system and coping resources in place to be able to navigate any potential negative consequences that may arise for sharing your story at this time and in this new way. If you don't quite have the support in place for taking on these risks, it may be wise to put a hold on sharing your story in this way until you're able to build up that support.

Even if you feel like now is the right time to share your story in a new way, it's helpful to plan some sort of "exit strategy" for how to retreat if you find yourself telling your story to a person, group, or forum, and the experience takes a negative turn. For example, you may want to plan in advance for how to change the subject, how to defer answering questions (e.g., "I'd prefer not to answer that question"), or how to exit the conversation or situation all together, such as wrapping up your speech early or leaving certain parts out. Most likely, people will be supportive and kind if they see you being vulnerable in sharing your story. However, sometimes, even well-meaning and kind-hearted people respond in ways that seem uncomfortable or offensive. Remember that protecting yourself in the process of sharing your story with others is an important act of self-care and healing.

With Whom to Tell Your Story

Here's an important point to remember: Not everyone is worthy of your story! You don't owe your story to anyone. Some people simply won't believe you, or they may judge or condemn you. This can happen even with people who are very close to you. I remember shortly after my own abusive relationship ended, I was talking with someone who up to that point in time I'd been very close to. As I was talking about the end of that relationship, I could hear the judgment in their voice, and they even clearly conveyed they weren't happy with me for making the choice to end that relationship. Looking back, I wish I would have had the inclination to simply end the conversation. Instead, since this person was so close to me and their opinion mattered a lot at that time, I felt compelled to try and convince them I'd made the right choice, so I shared more details of my former partner's abusive behaviors and told more of my story. Unfortunately, more details didn't do anything to change this person's mind, and I was left feeling even more frustrated and hurt by their response.

Sadly, you can't predict how someone will respond when you share your story with them, so any time you share your story with anyone, you're taking a huge risk you may be hurt in the process. Of course, the closer you are to someone and the more you know their character, the more likely you'll be able to imagine whether they'll be supportive. However, keep in mind that many people simply don't know a lot about abuse, and they may not know how to respond when they hear your story. Be thoughtful and intentional about who you share your story with—especially early in your healing journey. I think I would have had a much different response to the loved one I described above years after the relationship ended than I had so early in my healing journey since I was so emotional and in a state of turmoil at the time.

Be intentional with whom you share your story. Of course, trust your own instincts, but here are a few characteristics to look for in someone to entrust with your story (along with characteristics to alert you that a person may not be worthy of your story):

- Do you feel safe and comfortable with this person? (Or, do you feel uncomfortable or have a bad feeling about them?)
- Has this person demonstrated they are trustworthy? (Or, have they not taken steps toward building trust with you?)
- Has this person shown they can keep private information in confidence? (Or, are they known to gossip?)
- Does this person have good listening skills? (Or, do they tend to dominate conversations and make everything about them?)
- Will this person make time and space for you to share your story in a way that won't make you feel rushed? (Or, is this person too busy or rushed to devote their energy and attention to you?)

In addition to the above factors, think through what you know already about the person's views about abusive relationships. You may not know this directly, and if not, consider their views on related issues, such as women's rights, egalitarian relationships, marriage and relationships in general, and violence in general. Sometimes, people will surprise you — either positively or negatively — by having either more or less supportive responses to your story than you anticipated based on what you know about their value systems. However, people's values strongly influence their reactions. So, for example, let's say you know a family member's religious values are strongly opposed to divorce, and leaving your abusive relationship means ending your marriage. In this case, be prepared this family member may respond to your story with judgment or guidance about how to keep your marriage together, even if doing so puts your safety at risk.

Sometimes, people have unhelpful responses to hearing survivors' stories simply because they're misinformed about the nature of abuse. If you're sharing your story with someone who you generally know to be a kind, understanding person, and they offer a stigmatizing response, try and talk with them about how they've hurt or offended you. Some people still won't get it, but many good-hearted people will be willing to learn and correct how they respond in the future. On the other hand, if someone continues to be hurtful to you as you share parts of your story with them, remember you can stop sharing at any point in time. Again, you don't owe your story to anyone, and some people aren't worthy of hearing it.

The question with whom to share your story also applies to public forms of storytelling as you consider the audience to whom you'll be speaking. Think through the size of the crowd you'd feel comfortable with, as well as safety ramifications of a particular forum. Claim ownership of your process of sharing your story, and set boundaries with the people or organization with whom you're sharing your story. For example, if you're willing to share your story with the media, but you want to do so anonymously, don't let a reporter coax you into sharing more than you're comfortable with. Or, if you're speaking at a public event, let the organizers know what you are and are not comfortable with. You might let them know you want to read from a prepared script, or you might be comfortable taking open questions from the audience. If the organizers aren't willing to agree to honor your boundaries, it's okay to walk away from that opportunity and trust other opportunities will come your way another time.

Conclusion

Telling and retelling your story can be one of the most powerful parts of your journey of triumphing over abuse. However, it can be one of the scariest parts of that journey as well! This is especially true for public forms of storytelling, but there are risks that come with sharing your story more privately with a close friend or family member. In fact, those risks can feel even more frightening because you may risk being hurt or rejected by someone who means a lot to you. Every survivor's process and experiences of sharing their story is unique. Generally, it's wise to start with more private forms of storytelling earlier in the healing process, and then, if desired, move toward more public forums if that's something that appeals to you and is safe to do. Again, however, it's not a requirement to publicly share your story to be healed from abuse. Whether you decide to shout your story from the rooftops or keep your story private to only yourself, the process of telling and owning your story can be a powerful part of your healing process.

Most importantly, remember your story is still in progress. Your story isn't over. As you continue to triumph over abuse, continue to tell and retell your story in ways that make sense to you at the time. Consider your story as one that's still being written—and be sure to add your new experiences and growing wisdom and insights into your ever-unfolding story.

12
CONCLUSION
Beyond Survivorship

"Healing is ever-present, ever on-going, ever changing. I no longer believe I will ever say 'I am healed.' Rather, I believe I will always be saying 'I am healing.'"
~ Domestic Violence Survivor

As we come to the end of this book, know it's okay (and even expected) if you don't feel like you're anywhere near the end of your journey toward triumphing over abuse. We could probably debate whether the healing journey from abuse ever truly ends and whether there's such a thing as full and complete healing. My view is that each person's path is different. Some people will eventually feel like they've finally, fully healed from the abuse they experienced. For others, the healing process will be ongoing for the rest of their lives. As with all other aspects of this book, I invite you to come to your own conclusions about what your unique path will look like and where, if ever, it might end. Wherever your journey takes you, I hope this book has offered meaningful ideas about how to travel along the way there.

Throughout this book, we've covered many practical considerations regarding the process of healing from abuse. There are many steps you could take throughout this process, from building coping strategies and social support to changing harmful thought patterns and seeking professional counseling. In this final chapter, I'll turn attention to the more existential or spiritual dimensions of the triumphing process. To some extent, these dimensions are more complicated, but intentional self-reflection in these areas offers important insights to help you move forward in your healing journey and make sense of the difficult experiences you've faced. To conclude this book, I invite you to ponder the following five questions, and I'll start by saying the answers to these questions inherently can only be answered by you. I wish I could offer simple, practical steps for answering them, but in truth, these are questions that can only be answered through your own internal discovery process.

Question 1: Who Am I in Relation to My Abuse?

As we touched on in Chapter 1, even considering the words we use to describe people who've faced abuse is complicated. As I mentioned then, typically, I use the word *victim* to describe someone currently involved in a relationship with an abusive partner, and I use the word *survivor* to describe someone who formerly was involved with an abusive partner but who is no longer facing abuse within that relationship. As I've reflected on the meaning of these terms, I've often pondered the following question: If someone is first a *victim*, and then they become a *survivor*, then who do they become next after they've moved forward on their healing journey and no longer want to carry an identity related to their experiences with abuse? The best answer I've been able to come up with is they are who they have been all along: A human being with great potential to create a positive life for themselves and help others along the way.

As you move forward in your journey of triumphing over abuse, consider how you want to view your own identity, and whether you want to hold on to an identity connected to your experiences with abuse. Some people proudly wear the banner of "survivor" for the rest of their lives. Others prefer to eventually leave that identity behind. There are no right or wrong answers here, and it's up to you to consider what makes sense to you and how you want to view yourself and your experiences with abuse over the long-term trajectory of your life. Regardless of how you self-identify—even if right now you feel overwhelmed by your experiences and uncertain about what the future of your healing journey will look like—know that you are now, will be, and always have been more than your experiences of being abused.

Question 2: What Are the Unique Dreams I Have for My Future?

Give yourself freedom to dream about a brighter future in all areas of your life! Going through an abusive relationship usually entails setting aside your hopes and dreams, and often even involves losing in whole or in part a belief that you're worthy of a positive future. Although you share common experiences with others who've faced abuse, you also have your own unique path in life, and you'll make unique and important contributions to the world around you. What kind of future do you envision for yourself in 1 year, 5 years, 10 years, and even 20 or more years from now? It may feel overwhelming to think about this, especially if you're overwhelmed by the impacts of abuse on your life. One way to start is simply by talking about this with a supportive friend or family member or writing your thoughts in a journal. Start with your dreams, and then as your hopes and dreams become clearer, begin mapping out plans for the steps you can take to achieve this future vision for your life. Surround yourself with people who encourage you to keep these dreams alive and celebrate your successes as you move toward making those dreams a reality.

Question 3: How Can I Promote Safety in My Life so I Can Stay Free from Future Abuse and Build Healthy, Safe Relationships?

It's understandable to walk away from an abusive relationship and feel fear about letting other people get close to you. Your abuser was supposed to love and care for you, and instead they hurt you and tore you down. It's natural to come away from that experience with some scars and hesitation about letting other people get close to you. However, having close, healthy relationships with others (whether or not that includes a future romantic partner) is an important part of an overall happy, healthy life. And so, one deep struggle for many survivors is choosing to let people into your life, while also accepting the risk for potential hurt those relationships bring. Being hurt in relationships isn't an abstract theoretical concept for abuse survivors. When you've lived through abuse, you know how deeply the pain of hurt in a relationship can cut. As you explore the more existential aspects of your healing journey, I encourage you to dive deep into understanding your patterns in relationships, your perceptions of the risks and rewards in having close relationships with others, and what needs you have for connection that you risk trying to meet in unhealthy ways if you carry lingering hurts from your past abuse. This deeper exploration of the importance of safe, healthy relationships in your life can then help you identify and put in place proactive strategies for allowing these healthy relationships into your life, while also accepting and managing the potential risks that can come from relationship hurts.

Question 4: How Can I Make Sense of My Experiences? Why Did This All Happen to Me?

If you're like me, one of the major questions you ask yourself about the difficult experiences in your life is, "Why?" Why did you have to go through it? Why did that person hurt you in that way? Why do good people have to have such bad things happen to them? Many of these questions simply may never be able to be answered with complete certainty. If it's helpful to you to try and make sense of unanswerable questions, then spend some time doing so. For example, you may never know for sure why your abuser hurt you, but it's possible you could find likely answers by considering their past history, understanding their personality, and examining how social systems and institutions perpetuate abuse. However, it also may be worth simply trying to accept you can never truly know the answers to these questions. Your religious or spiritual beliefs may help you understand these questions more fully, or at least have faith to know you don't need to have all of the answers to be able to trust there can be some greater purpose through even the most difficult experiences. It can be helpful to acknowledge there are some things that simply don't make sense, such as what might drive one person to deeply hurt another person. And yet, even in these most difficult situations, there can be some greater purpose or meaning to them, whether in your own life, in the lives of others, or in the larger community. As best you can, consider how you can make sense of your experiences in a way that helps you continue moving forward in your healing journey, even if sometimes that means acknowledging you might never fully understand why those experiences happened.

Question 5: How Can I Keep Growing, Healing, and Learning for the Rest of My Life?

Personal growth and development are lifelong processes. Of course, self-development is important to balance with self-acceptance just as you are now. However, if you want to continue to grow and learn for the rest of your life, know you can do so in ways that are meaningful to you. Spend time in deep reflection considering not only what dreams you hold for your future life—such as your career, future relationships, and experiences like traveling—but also what your vision is for becoming an even better of yourself with each passing day, month, and year. Allow your experiences with abuse to be a catalyst toward learning to approach life with curiosity and an eagerness to learn and grow. But don't just do this because I'm recommending it—consider what that commitment to growth means to you, especially in the context of your experiences of surviving abuse. In your abusive relationship, your abuser likely limited your ability to grow and become who you're meant to be. Now that you're free from that relationship, you're also free to make decisions about how you want to experience your future, and what characteristics, opportunities, and mindsets you might need to develop to make that future vision of yourself a reality. Plan opportunities to regularly check in on your growth and progress, such as by keeping a journal to update regularly. Don't forget to celebrate your progress and look back on how far you've come. It can be easy to forget where you used to be as you move forward into who you're becoming. With each new day, however, you have opportunities to keep growing and learning in ways you might never have imagined while you were facing abuse.

Conclusion: My Wish for You

I'm deeply grateful you chose to read this book as part of your journey toward healing from past abuse. I hope this book offered you new ideas about ways to approach your recovery process, as well as that the information we've discussed helps you activate new steps in your journey toward healing and triumphing over past abuse. My wish for you is that you know that you're not alone, that you're not to blame for the abuse you've experienced, and that you're worthy of healing and a positive life. Also, I encourage you to connect with meaningful relationships and communities to support you in your healing journey. We'd love for you to join us in the See the Triumph community (www.seethetriumph.org) if you're not already connected with us there!

I also hope you've embraced your healing journey as an opportunity to dream about a positive future, and that it *is* possible to achieve your dreams. You are deserving of a happy, healthy life—no matter what anyone has said to you, done to you, or made you believe about yourself. You *can* triumph over abuse, and in fact, my guess is, you're already well on your way.

Index